Individual Rights and Civic Responsibility

THE RIGHT TO PRIVACY

Brandon Garrett

The Rosen Publishing Group, Inc.
New York

Published in 2001 by The Rosen Publishing Group, Inc.
29 East 21st Street, New York, NY 10010

Cover image: The Constitution of the United States of America

Library of Congress Cataloging-in-Publication Data

Garrett, Brandon
  The right to privacy / Brandon Garrett.—1st ed.
      p.   cm. (Individual rights and civic responsibility)
  Includes bibliographical references and index.
      ISBN 0-8239-3236-2
  1. Privacy, Right of—United States—Juvenile literature. [1.
Privacy, Right of.] I. Title. II. Series
    KF1262.Z9 G37 2000
    342.73'0858—dc21

                                                  00-010507

About the Author

Brandon Garrett earned a B.A. in philosophy from Yale University and worked as an advocate for homeless people in New York before attending law school at Columbia University. He was born in Maryland.

To Mom, Dad, and Nat

Contents

Introduction:
What Is the Right to Privacy?

The stores where you shop are monitored by video cameras. Your school principal can ask that your belongings be searched for drugs. Police can get permission to search your home. Your telephone conversations can be recorded, and records are kept of every number that you call. Are you ever really alone?

Privacy can mean keeping information to ourselves. It can also mean being left alone at times, and being free from others interfering in our lives. Justice Louis D. Brandeis famously called the right to privacy "the right to be let alone."

But do you always want to be alone? If no one is watching you, then no one is protecting you either. The government may want to watch us for our own protection. The government has the greatest power to invade our privacy, since the government controls the police and other officials that can use force against us. On the other hand, government force is also intended to protect us. Without some limits, though, people fear that the government could abuse the trust that we place in it to limit our privacy only when necessary for the public good. The right to privacy can be a protection against having a society in which the government completely controls our lives. For instance, in many societies around the world, the police can interfere with people's daily lives without restrictions, and people live in constant fear of being watched. Ideally, the right to privacy protects us from having the government control areas of our lives that are important to our freedom and our individuality.

What does it mean to be let alone? Let alone in what ways? The word "privacy" is very vague because there are so many things in our daily lives that we cannot keep to ourselves and yet many other things that we want to keep private. What information is most important to keep private? The things that many of us consider private or personal include our thoughts, our conversations with others, our intimate relationships, and maybe even our personal belongings. We want the government and other people to respect our right to keep some of these things to ourselves. Beliefs about what we should be allowed to keep private differ from person to person. These beliefs reflect our values and may be influenced by our cultural background or religion. Attitudes about privacy have certainly changed over time. For example, today, when many young Americans grow up with their own rooms, or share rooms separate from their parents, we take the value of our personal space for granted. We value personal space much more than Americans did when almost everyone lived in a one- or two-room home.

What Are Rights?

Rights are entitlements that belong to everyone as a matter of law. Legal rights give us the ability to challenge the actions of others in a court. Rights can be given to us by a law passed by the state we live in, by Congress, or by the Constitution, which is the supreme law of the United States. Often a law or a section of the Constitution is unclear, in which case a court must decide how to interpret important rights. In some cases, rights may conflict with each other. For example, if someone wants to write about your personal life, your right to privacy might conflict with that person's right to free speech. The way the law defines the right to privacy may influence people's values and views about privacy. Having a legal right gives people a way to have their rights vindicated in a court, and it also deters people from violating people's privacy in the first place.

Where Does the Right to Privacy Come From?

The right to privacy is a child of the twentieth century, a new right that is constantly changing and being defined. We will see how the meaning of certain rights can change and grow. The idea of a new right may seem very strange, but we will see that the law is always changing.

The right to privacy is unusual in that the word "privacy" is not ever mentioned in the Constitution. Nor is privacy ever mentioned in the Bill of Rights, which is a series of ten amendments that were the first to be added to the Constitution. The

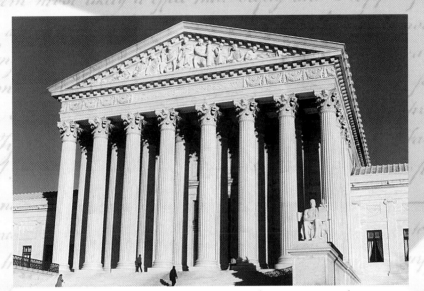

An important part of the Supreme Court's job is to interpret the Constitution and the Bill of Rights.

right to privacy is interesting because in some ways, it is nowhere but everywhere. Privacy is not mentioned in the Bill of Rights, but privacy is an important part of many of the other rights that are guaranteed in those constitutional amendments. Privacy is relevant to the right to freedom from unreasonable searches and seizures, the right to remain silent, the right to counsel, the right to freedom of association, and other rights that we will explain in this book.

We will also discuss the role of the highest court in America, the Supreme Court. An important—perhaps the most important—part of the Supreme Court's job is to interpret the Constitution and explain what the rights defined in it really mean. The Court has interpreted the Bill of Rights as guaranteeing and protecting several fundamental rights, some of which are not specifically mentioned in the Bill of Rights. For example, the Court interprets the Bill of Rights as protecting privacy, but only specific kinds of privacy, including privacy regarding a woman's decision to obtain an abortion, and privacy in matters involving reproduction, family decisions, and marriage.

In addition to the Constitution itself, many important state and federal laws exist that protect our privacy. Laws protect information in schools, work records, and other kinds of private information. In many ways, the right to privacy is a battleground. New laws are constantly being proposed to protect privacy rights or to take them away.

Privacy issues can become very controversial and touch on some of the most important ideas and debates in society today. Some things are important for the government to know, even if they seem personal or private. Police are permitted to listen to private telephone conversations to solve an important crime, but only if they receive a proper warrant from a judge. People are in disagreement about why and when the government should be able to interfere with the privacy of its citizens. For example, for many years courts and police refused to do anything about family violence and permitted people to abuse their children or their spouses without arresting them or preventing them from hurting family members. The justification was that family matters are private. Today, however, police do arrest people who abuse family members, and the law says that there is nothing private about violence, nor is violence only a family matter.

Not only does the right to privacy mean that the government must let us alone in some areas, but many laws also require the government to make sure that our privacy is not invaded by other people, organizations, or corporations. Some would like the government to actively prevent other people from interfering with our privacy. New forms of technology make intrusions into people's private lives easier. A great deal of private information is available electronically, and whenever people buy something at a store or see a doctor or use a computer, they are often unwittingly releasing private information to outsiders. Many new laws are being considered to prevent private companies from recovering private information that can be obtained electronically, often over the Internet.

1 History of the Right to Privacy

Privacy is part of a culture, so as a culture's values change, ideas about privacy also change. The very idea of a private life is in many ways a modern concept.

Early History

Many of the things that we take for granted as part of our private lives were not kept private two hundred years ago in colonial America. Colonial homes tended to be small, with few rooms and thin walls and floors. Keeping conversations private was difficult because members of a family often slept and lived in the same room. Only toward the beginning of the eighteenth century, when hallways became more common and rooms were no longer attached, was there more privacy in the home. In some ways, however, people had more privacy in the past; there were few newspapers or reporters, and solitude was easy to find because there were fewer cities.

Privacy was an important concern after the American Revolution. Many states demanded that some individual rights be guaranteed in the new Constitution before they were willing to endorse it. In response to these demands, the Bill of Rights was ratified in 1791. These amendments to the Constitution limited the power of the federal government (but not, at that time, the power of the state governments) to take certain actions affecting people's rights. Although the right to privacy is not discussed in the Bill of Rights, many of the provisions of the Bill of Rights involve privacy issues. Privacy involves freedom from government intrusion into one's daily life, and the people who wrote the Constitution, sometimes called the framers of the Constitution, were very concerned about these kinds of intrusions.

The framers were particularly concerned with the right to privacy in one's own home. One of the most resented practices of the British troops stationed in the colonies before the Revolution was the practice of quartering. The Quartering Act of 1774 gave British troops the authority to force colonists to quarter British troops in their homes and provide them with food and lodging for free. The British could then take over a person's house whenever they so desired. In 1774, the British stationed their troops in Boston because they were concerned that the colonists were becoming disobedient. The people of Boston severely resented having to quarter the British troops, especially since they did not want them in their town in the first place.

The Third Amendment addresses this special concern about standing armies, or armies that are kept in peacetime, and the fear that people might have to feed and care for an army during times when it is not really needed. This amendment was written because of the colonists' outrage against the practice of quartering, and some people call this amendment the "Quartering Amendment." The Third Amendment says:

> No Soldier shall, in time of peace be quartered in any house, without the consent of the Owner, nor in time of war, but in a manner to be prescribed by law.

The Third Amendment has never been a real issue, since there has never been a need for our own troops to be stationed in peoples' houses in our own country, but it shows that the framers of the Constitution had very important privacy concerns in their day and were willing to be very specific to be sure that those violations of privacy would never occur again in the new republic that they were creating. The amendment shows that at that time privacy in their own homes was particularly important to Americans.

The Fourth Amendment to the Constitution was also written to address intrusions into personal space. The Fourth Amendment says:

> The right of the people to be secure in their persons, houses, papers, and effects, against unreasonable searches and seizures, shall not be violated, and no Warrants shall issue, but upon probable cause, supported by Oath or affirmation, and particularly describing the place to be searched, and the persons or things to be seized.

The Fourth Amendment is about privacy in the home, but it is also about privacy from searches by officials like the police. Because of the Fourth Amendment, police must obtain a warrant before searching any person or person's home. A judge can issue the warrant only if there is "probable cause," and if the police obtain the warrant, they can search only for specific things. In addition, the courts have interpreted what it means for a search to be "unreasonable." For example, when police read someone his or her rights, they are following a rule that was established in the Supreme Court case of *Miranda v. Arizona*, where the Court said that a reasonable search under the Fourth Amendment requires the person who is being searched to be told about his or her rights under the Constitution.

Another place in the Bill of Rights where people have located a right to privacy is the Ninth Amendment. The Ninth Amendment says:

The enumeration in the Constitution, of certain rights, shall not be construed to deny or disparage others retained by the people.

This means that people have other rights not specifically named in the Bill of Rights. Some believe that the right to privacy is or should be one of these unnamed rights that belong to the people. Other people believe that the Ninth Amendment is too vague. What does it mean, to say that the people have many other rights? Some say that if we took the Ninth Amendment to heart, we could invent any right we chose and call it a right "retained by the people." The framers of the Constitution may have just meant to say that the rights that had existed traditionally up to that time are to be kept, or retained, by the people. For example, if under traditional,

15

common law, you can sue a person who intrudes into your private life, you can still do so even if the Bill of Rights never talks about things as specific as those kinds of lawsuits.

History of Privacy Before and After the Civil War

One very important thing to remember about the Bill of Rights is that it applied only to the new federal government and not to the states. The federal government could not make unreasonable searches and seizures or quarter troops, but the states were restricted only by their own laws and constitutions. The states were worried about national, or federal, power and so they sought to preserve, and not limit, their own power.

After the Civil War, the Fourteenth Amendment was passed. The Fourteenth Amendment guarantees equal protection under the law and due process for all citizens. Later, courts interpreted this guarantee as making the Bill of Rights a limit on the states, just as it originally limited the federal government.

Applying privacy rights against the states that were regularly abusing those rights was a hard-fought and important accomplishment. Many of the objectives of the antislavery, abolitionist movement and later the civil rights movement were concerned with providing privacy rights that had up until that time been denied to blacks. The southern states did not respect the privacy of black slaves, since they did not really even acknowledge that slaves were human. Southern judges said that blacks were

Before the Civil War, southern states went to great lengths to prevent potential slave revolts. Police would search homes to see if fugitive slaves were being harbored, limiting the right to privacy.

not "persons" so they could not enjoy any of the protections of the law. Southern states passed laws called "black codes," which severely restricted the activities of blacks. Slaves could not marry, could not own land, could not earn wages; they could not testify in court against whites and could be punished with death for the most minor acts. Teaching a slave to read was classified as a crime. Slaves could never control their living conditions, and their lives were completely under the control of their owners. Slaves therefore had no right to privacy because they had no rights at all.

Southern states, knowing the cruelty that they inflicted upon black slaves, were afraid of slave revolts and used a series of limits on the right to privacy to make sure that no revolts would occur. They went to great lengths to force northerners to return fugitive slaves who had fled to the North. Northern states would use police to search home after home to see if they were hiding fugitive slaves. These searches severely limited privacy of the home. The southern states searched the mail and read private letters for signs of abolitionist activity and regularly seized pamphlets promoting abolitionist views.

After the Civil War, in 1865, the northern states forced the former Confederate states to accept new amendments to the Constitution as a condition for rejoining the Union. The Thirteenth Amendment prohibited slavery, or involuntary servitude. And as we discussed, the Fourteenth Amendment guaranteed equal protection under the law and due process to all persons born in the United States. This meant that for the first time, the Fourth Amendment applied to the states as well as to the federal government, and from that time the states could not conduct unreasonable searches and seizures. The Fourteenth Amendment also says that the law must be applied equally. For example, if the police search only blacks, then the police are acting unreasonably and are not treating all citizens as equals.

The passing of the Fourteenth Amendment was a high watermark for civil rights, but the southern states soon eroded its power by enacting laws that restricted the freedom of the newly freed slaves, or freedmen. These laws were nicknamed Jim Crow, and they created a segregated society in which blacks were forced to be separated from whites in public and private places. Blacks could not ride in the same train cars, live in the same neighborhoods, go to the same schools, or eat at the same restaurants as whites. Blacks could not marry whites, and "grandfather" clauses, or unfair taxes and tests, were used to prevent blacks from registering to vote.

When rights were denied, whether by the British or by southern whites, privacy rights were often the first to go. Privacy rights were denied to blacks as part of Jim Crow. By the 1880s, southerners had unleashed a campaign of violence designed to make blacks so afraid for their lives that they would not even try to gain full rights. Lynchings occurred frequently—gangs of whites would form large mobs and publicly attack and kill blacks. Often these white mobs were encouraged by local police. Very little privacy existed for blacks then, and if you were black, police could arrest you for sitting in the wrong place or for being seen with whites. The police were always watching to see whether blacks crossed any of the lines that kept them in a subordinated position. Obviously, very little security can exist in your home if mobs can attack at any time and the police will not provide you with any protection.

Real privacy and security for African Americans and other minorities have come slowly. Almost a hundred years after the Civil War, in 1964, a Civil Rights Act was passed guaranteeing all people equal access to public accommodations like restaurants and theaters and buses. But as we will see in later sections of this book, problems with the police and with racism still exist. In their efforts to stop crimes from happening, police my harass or stop people just because of their race. In practice, privacy rights still depend on what color you are in many parts of America.

The Beginnings of a Right to Privacy

A lawyer named Louis Brandeis, who later became a Supreme Court justice, is thought to have been the first to coin the phrase "right to privacy." While privacy is an important part of many of the constitutional amendments that made up the Bill of Rights, Brandeis was the first to argue that it should be a right on its own.

In 1890, with his law partner Samuel D. Warren, Brandeis wrote a famous law article called "The Right to Privacy." Brandeis and Warren complained in their article that the press was publishing too much private information about people's personal affairs, and they put forth the idea that people should have the right to sue if their privacy was interfered with. Brandeis wrote:

> Instantaneous photographs and newspaper enterprise have invaded the sacred precincts of private and domestic life; and numerous mechanical devices threaten to make good the prediction that what is whispered in the closet shall be

proclaimed from the housetops. The press is overstepping in every direction the obvious bounds of propriety and decency. Gossip is no longer the resource of the idle and the vicious, but has become a trade.

This sounds just like the complaints of today's public figures and celebrities that cameras and tabloids are following them everywhere. Today, technology has made eavesdropping and taking photos of people's private lives easier than ever. Of course, people always lose some privacy if they choose to be in the spotlight. But how about the privacy of people who never wanted any attention in the first place, and simply want to be left alone?

Brandeis argued that although the right to privacy was a new right, there was a basis for the right in traditional law. He said that courts should recognize the right to privacy as a matter of common law. What does that mean? The oldest source of law in the United States is the common law, the name for the law that we Americans inherited from the British. The common law originated in the time of William the Conqueror, and it was part of an effort by the king of England to make all citizens follow one law, or a common law. This English common law has always been a law of precedent, which means that judges must follow the decisions laid down in cases that have come before. The common law changes only when judges decide they must make a new rule to explain how a new case fits with the old decisions, or if after many years judges determine that the old rules are obsolete. The common law was made by judges very slowly over the years and eventually developed into a large body of law. The American colonies adopted

Celebrities and public figures sacrifice some of their right to privacy for life in the spotlight.

the English common law as their law when the United States won its independence because colonists were used to the British laws. Adopting British law was easier than trying to completely rewrite all of the laws on the books. Since that time, though, American judges have taken the old British rules and changed them over the years. Brandeis believed that a right to privacy should be recognized as part of this common law collection of rules because it protected people from harm in the same way that many cases that had become part of common law already did.

Brandeis also recognized that the right to privacy has its limits, and he developed some of the themes that have been important in discussions of the right to privacy ever since. He said that there should be a general right to privacy, but that the government should be able to limit that right when it is in the public interest. He distinguished between a "legitimate concern" and "unwarranted invasion" into people's private lives. As we will see, it is very hard to draw the lines that decide what should be kept private and what is a strong enough public interest to justify limiting people's privacy.

Courts would only slowly develop this idea that people have a right to privacy. In an early case in 1902 called *Robertson v. Rochester Folding Box Co.*, a flour company had used a picture of a pretty young girl on their flour boxes. The problem was that the picture was of a real girl, and the flour company had never asked for her permission. She said that she was emotionally traumatized by having her image on all those flour boxes, and that she was "greatly humiliated by the scoffs and jeers of persons who ha[d] recognized her face." She sued for damages to compensate her for her emotional distress. The court said that there was no such thing as a right to privacy and disparaged Brandeis's "clever article." Not only did the court not let a jury decide whether the girl should receive any compensation, but the court said that she did not even have a right to sue in the first place. The legal term for a right to sue is a "cause of action," and the court said that she did not even have a cause of action because no other court had ever recognized a right to privacy.

Many people were upset by the decision in *Robertson v. Rochester Folding Box Co.*, and in the next year, the New York State legislature passed a law saying that no one can use the name or image of a person without his or her permission. The New York law also created a cause of action, so that if someone violates the law, the victim has the right to sue in court. This law was the very first American law written to protect a right to privacy, and it was a state law. Federal laws, which apply to all of the states, would come much later. But by the 1920s and 1930s, this idea of a right to privacy began to take hold in several other states.

New laws and court decisions said that people could sue newspapers for publishing embarrassing private material, even if it were true. This was the very practice that Brandeis complained about in his article. This meant that the right to privacy conflicted with the First Amendment right to freedom of the press. Courts later began to limit the right to privacy, in order to protect newspapers from being sued so often that they might become afraid to provide useful or important information to the public. Some cases bring up very complex ethical issues for a newspaper editor who must decide how much information to include in a story.

Newspapers must determine whether reporting embarrassing private information about a public figure serves the public interest.

Like many other areas of the law, when we think about privacy rights, we must balance private rights against the public interest. On the one hand, newspapers serve an important public purpose in reporting the news, even if it is scandalous; newspapers inform the public and help people understand current events. On the other hand, some information might not have enough educational value to justify the harm that it might cause to a person's reputation. Also, the possibility of discrimination becomes a concern if newspapers are allowed to selectively decide whose reputation matters less and whose matters more, or to otherwise infringe upon individuals' privacy in a biased manner. For example, should a newspaper be able to show footage of a person engaging in offensive behavior—for example, being drunk and disorderly in public? Or does such footage have no real newsworthy purpose and serve only to embarrass the person?

The Right to Privacy

Newspapers are sometimes confronted with information about the private sexual lives of politicians. Should newspapers hesitate to publicize stories about the marital infidelities of prominent politicians? Does such information serve any socially valuable purpose? Is there any tasteful way to print such stories? Do public figures voluntarily surrender their privacy when they decide to put themselves in the spotlight to begin with?

Should local newspapers be more careful than larger newspapers or television stations about using people's names in stories that may affect their private lives? Have you ever had your name used in an article in a newspaper, and if so, do you think that your name was used accurately and fairly?

Newspapers do not disclose the names of minors who are accused of committing crimes, to protect their privacy. Do you think that this is a good idea? Would you want to know if a classmate was accused of committing a particular crime? Would you want your name published if you were accused of a crime?

Many newspapers do not report the names of rape victims in order to protect their privacy and emotional well-being. Rape is so traumatic that many victims find it too difficult to even discuss the crime. There is some concern that if newspapers could report the names of victims, many victims would not report crimes to the police. Some states, including Florida, have passed laws requiring newspapers to keep the names of rape victims anonymous. However, the Supreme Court, in a 1989 case called *The Florida Star v. B.J.F.*, said that because it was the police department that gave the newspaper the information, and

Louis D. Brandeis (1856–1941)

The first article defending privacy rights, indeed the first to even call privacy a right, was written by a young Boston lawyer named Louis Brandeis, along with his partner, Samuel D. Warren, in 1890. Brandeis would make privacy rights and progressive social activism the hallmarks of his incredible legal career. As a lawyer he was a crusader, known as a "peoples lawyer," representing small corporations against large monopolies, and campaigning for minimum wages, shorter workdays for workers, especially women and children, and public land conservation. He became one of the most famous lawyers of his day, arguing before the Supreme Court that even if there was not strong legal support for the idea that women and children should be protected from long work hours, economic and social data proved that it was harmful. He won, and to this day legal briefs that use scientific data are called Brandeis briefs.

He was appointed to the Supreme Court in 1916–the first Jew to be a Supreme Court justice. Many anti-Semites vigorously opposed his appointment, despite his record. As a justice, Brandeis authored many of the century's most famous opinions. He defined the right to privacy as "the right to be let alone" in his dissenting opinion in *Olmstead v. United States* in 1928. This was the first case involving wiretapping to be heard by the Court, and he argued that wiretapping violated privacy rights. The Supreme Court finally came around to his position, quoting Brandeis's article in 1967 in *Katz v. United States*, finally holding that the Fourth Amendment does protect against eavesdropping, and his language from *Olmstead* has been relied upon in hundreds of opinions since.

27

because the law applied only to small neighborhood newspapers, the law was invalid. However, the Court ruled to allow some limits on what kinds of information newspapers can publish.

These examples show how privacy rights generate controversy, and how the courts have gone back and forth as they seek to define the appropriate balance between a newspaper's right to free speech and an individual's right to privacy.

Intrusion into Private Life

By the late 1960s, courts began to realize not only that invasion of privacy is very serious, but also that privacy can be violated even if nobody ever actually obtains any personal information. People can still feel that their privacy is being taken away if they are subjected to constant prying, or annoying, but failed, efforts to obtain personal information. Some courts have recognized that people should be able to sue if they are subjected to especially severe intrusion into their privacy.

In one famous case, Ralph Nader, the famous writer, advocate for consumer safety, and presidential candidate was targeted by General Motors after he began to speak out and question the safety of G.M. cars, especially a Chevrolet car called the Corvair, which he argued was a deathtrap. He was about to publish a book about the Corvair, *Unsafe at Any Speed*, that would eventually cause a national outcry over auto safety and become a bestseller. G.M. was determined to stop him and hired private detectives to follow him in public, make harassing phone calls, and inquire into his private views and private life. Nader sued and G.M. eventually paid him $425,000 to settle the case and denied any wrongdoing.

In another troubling case, a doctor insisted upon taking photographs of a dying patient. The patient objected by clenching his fist and shaking his head. The court in *Bethiume v. Pratt* (1976) decided that even though those photographs were never printed, the dead man's family could receive compensation because he had a right not to be photographed.

Stealing Your Identity

People still sometimes sue when their images are used in advertisements, just like the girl on the flour box. Some of these cases seem outrageous, since many of the people depicted in the advertisements are famous figures whose personalities are already public. Vanna White, from the television show *Wheel of Fortune*, recently sued Samsung Electronics when it used her image in an ad. But did Samsung really use her image? Samsung's ad showed a robot wearing a wig, a dress, and jewelry like those that Vanna White wears. The robot was standing just like Vanna White does, next to letters on a game board that looked just like the *Wheel of Fortune* game board. The Supreme Court, in *White v. Samsung Electronics* (1992) said that since the advertisement was not actually a picture of her, her right to privacy was not violated. This means that advertisements can use imitations of celebrities as long as they do not use actual images. Do you think a celebrity should be able to stop advertisements that use impersonators making fun of them?

3 Police Searches and Seizures

While a general right to privacy has been recognized only in a few areas related to family life, certain kinds of privacy are recognized in the Constitution. As we discussed, the Fourth Amendment to the Constitution establishes a right to be safe from police activity that interferes with our private lives. Police cannot enter our homes without a warrant signed by a judge or engage in "unreasonable searches and seizures."

From early times, the right to privacy has been connected with having a right to be left alone by the authorities, especially the police. The police have so much power to enter our private lives that it is especially important to limit their actions. And although police have a great deal of power, the Constitution also limits everything that police do in their daily work.

The Fourth Amendment prevents the police or other government agents from making an unreasonable search or seizure. You may have heard that police must have a warrant signed by a judge and "probable cause" to make an arrest. Police must have probable cause to believe that someone is engaging in or about to engage in a specific kind of criminal behavior. Probable cause is also described as enough information to lead a reasonable person to believe that a crime has occurred.

Courts have also said that if the police have a "reasonable suspicion" that someone is engaging in criminal activity or is about to do so, they can "stop and frisk" that individual. For example, although the police may not have full probable cause to think that a man is about to shoot someone just because there is a bulge in his jacket, they might have a pretty reasonable suspicion that he is carrying a gun. They can pat him down to check for any concealed weapons, a process that is humiliating and that can also become violent. The police can conduct a full search if they discover a weapon in a frisk, since they then have full probable cause.

In some situations, searches can even be performed with no suspicion at all, if and when important public safety issues are involved. Airline pilots and train operators can be given drug tests without any suspicion because so many lives depend on safe transportation. Do you think that random drug testing is justified by the concern over public safety?

Some state courts protect people against searches more than the Supreme Court does under the U.S. Constitution. For example, New York State requires two more levels of suspicion, in addition to probable cause and reasonable suspicion. Most police departments are operated by a local, municipal, or city government, or by a county. A local police department may have its own rules and regulations regarding stops that are made. Sometimes, because of lawsuits, courts require police

If you are stopped by the police and run away or physically resist a search, you may be charged with a crime.

departments to follow a set of rules when they make stops that protect a citizen's privacy more fully than the Constitution does.

What to Do If You Are Stopped by the Police

More and more youth are being stopped by police and then treated as adult criminals instead of within the juvenile justice system. Some minors are now being given the death sentence, sentences are being made harsher, and adult sentencing is being used more, even in juvenile courts. The emphasis is on punishing young people, and not on helping minors deal with problems and become responsible adults.

If you should ever be stopped by the police, it is important that you don't ever resist a search in any physical way. Resisting arrest is usually a crime. At most, state that you do not consent to the search, loudly and clearly, so that others nearby can hear you. Later on, you can make a complaint or take action against the police if they violate your rights, but do not try to vindicate your rights in person.

Do not run from the police. According to a recent Supreme Court case, *Whren v. United States* (1999), running from the police can itself be grounds for police suspicion and can lead to a police stop. Do not turn around, since the officer might think you are reaching for a weapon. Stand perfectly still. Try not to panic. Stay relaxed.

Keep your hands in plain sight. Do not make any fast motions with your hands. People have been killed because officers thought that they were reaching for guns. In a tense

33

situation, especially at night, any movement could be mistaken for reaching for a gun, so do not make any rapid motions and keep your hands out in plain sight.

Try your best to answer calmly any questions that the police ask. Be polite, allow the officer to speak, and address him or her as "officer." Try not to show nervousness, frustration, and most important, do not be rude or abrasive.

Tell the police officer your name and your address, because otherwise—since the police will not be able to find you later—the police will arrest you. Remember that police officers may not be experienced, are only trying to do their job, and may be tense because they themselves are afraid.

If you are ever stopped by the police, you have the right to remain silent. You do not need to speak if police officers ask questions that you do not want to answer about what you are doing or about anything that could make them suspect you of a crime. You should remain silent until you have a chance to talk to your parents or a lawyer. Use your judgment; if the situation is easy to resolve, it may be wise to talk to the officers about what happened and to clear up any misunderstanding. Giving them the information they ask for may end the encounter quickly. But if there is any chance that you are under suspicion of a crime or a violation, for your own protection you should remain silent, even if the police try to pressure you into talking to them. Remember that anything that you say can be used in court.

If you are stopped by the police and believe that your rights have been violated, try to remember the names of the officers, their badge numbers, the license plate number of the patrol car, and the place and time of the incident so that, if necessary, you can make a complaint in the future. Many police departments have civilian complaint review procedures, under which you can take confidential action against an officer who abuses your rights. If you believe your rights have been violated, you may want to file this type of confidential complaint so that the police department can hold officers accountable and prevent them from engaging in abusive behavior. If the police department is not responsive to your complaint, you can also contact a community group that may be able to complain on your behalf or give you other ways to make your story heard.

Police Brutality

Abusive searches are not reasonable searches. However, in many well-publicized cases, police officers have gone so far as to shoot unarmed civilians and claim that they were afraid for their lives and had reasonable grounds to use deadly force. Police are allowed to use whatever force is necessary to restrain a person for an arrest, so resisting police with force can escalate an encounter. Resisting police, even verbally, is a dangerous idea. If you ever have an encounter with the police, even though you may be anxious or afraid, keeping calm is extremely important. Police may be poorly trained or new recruits. They may be as afraid of you as you are of them. Do not let them overreact and resort to violence; move very slowly and talk clearly so that there are no misunderstandings.

Young people are the victims of police brutality more often than any other age group. Why do you think that is the case? Part of the reason may be fear on the part of the officers. Do you think that the perception that young men are dangerous is part of a stereotype—a stereotype that can have deadly consequences? If you are interested in police brutality issues, one group you can contact is the October 22nd Coalition to Stop Police Brutality, Repression and the Criminalization of a Generation, P.O. Box 2627, New York, NY, 10009 (http://www.unstoppable.com/22/). The group publishes and sells a book called *Stolen Lives—Killed by Law Enforcement*, which tells the stories of people, many of whom were teenagers, who have been killed by the police in America.

Juvenile Curfews

Jessica is a sixteen-year-old high school student. After finishing a study session at the home of one of her classmates, she begins walking home at 11:15 PM.

Fifteen-year-old Jacob has arrived home from the school dance just before his 11:00 PM parental curfew. Jacob is hungry and asks for his parents' permission to go with "the guys" to McDonald's for a burger. His parents consent and wave to him from the doorway as he gets into the backseat of his friend's car.

James, a sixteen-year-old aspiring musician, is driving home at 12:05 AM after finishing a benefit gig with his band at the neighborhood youth center.

Michael, a fifteen-year-old high school swimmer, is up at 5:00 AM, dressed, and bicycling down the sidewalk at 5:30 AM to get to swim practice on time.

These vignettes, or ones very similar to them, play out in families night after night, in town after town, across the United States. What may distinguish one town from another, however, is whether or not the town has enacted a juvenile curfew ordinance that criminally proscribes the activities of teenagers even if they have parental consent, as recounted in the previous vignettes. In those municipalities that choose to enact juvenile curfew ordinances, the typical consequences of the seemingly innocent activities of Jessica, Jacob, James, and Michael might be arrest, overnight detention, suspension of driving privileges, or community service hours. Their parents might face a criminal fine, community service hours, and/or parenting classes.

Juvenile curfew laws pose one of the most serious threats to the constitutional rights of young adults. Although curfew laws have been around for a hundred years, they have mostly been used only in temporary emergencies. Today, juvenile curfews are becoming increasingly popular and common, especially in communities that are concerned about gang violence. These curfew laws usually say that minors under the age of sixteen cannot be outside their homes after a certain hour at night, usually eleven o'clock, and if they are caught, they face overnight detention, suspension of driving privileges, community service hours, or even arrest.

Curfew laws are passed by cities or counties out of fear of juvenile crime, to protect juveniles from crime, and to support parents' authority over their children. These are understandable concerns, and these laws keep getting passed. On the other hand, no studies have shown any sure connection between these laws and an actual reduction in juvenile crime. The fact is, the people fined or arrested under the curfew laws are not guilty of any crime, only of being outside. Some of the laws do not even create an exception when children have permission from their parents to stay outside, though most say that being outside with an adult is allowed. Not only do the laws infringe upon the rights of minors, but they may limit parents' rights to raise their children as they see fit. Do you think that your parents would support a curfew law?

There is also a serious concern that police will enforce these curfew laws in a discriminatory way, arresting only minority children or poor children after hours. Some of these laws give police a great deal of discretion in deciding whether to fine minors, accept an excuse, take them to a special juvenile curfew center, or arrest them. Police already arrest far more minority children than nonminority children, and minority children receive far harsher sentences than nonminorities who commit the same offenses. A curfew law gives police greater discretion and may also give them more opportunity to display bias and discrimination.

A good example of how the courts treat curfew laws was demonstrated by a recent federal lawsuit, *Hutchins v. District of Columbia*, which involved a curfew law in the District of Columbia. The law prohibits minors under the age of seventeen from being in public areas unaccompanied by an assigned adult of at least twenty-one years of age from 11:00 PM to 6:00 AM Sunday through Thursday, and from 12:01 AM to 6:00 AM on Friday and Saturday. Nine children and four parents sued, arguing that the law restricted the rights of free movement, free speech, freedom of assembly, and the right to be free from unreasonable searches and seizures. The court balanced the rights of minors against the interest of the district in protecting minors from harm, and upheld the law, saying that the state has a broad authority over children, and that this law was not too vague.

The Supreme Court has repeatedly decided not to review lower court decisions upholding similar juvenile curfew laws. However, the Court has found a similar kind of law unconstitutional—an antiloitering law that prohibited remaining in one place outside at any time of day. In *City of Chicago v. Morales* (1999), the Supreme Court struck down a Chicago antiloitering law that let police walk up to groups of people who were outside, tell them to disperse, and—if they were still there after fifteen minutes—arrest them. The law basically made it a crime to stand outside with others for longer than fifteen minutes. The law was very popular among crime-fearing Chicago residents. They thought it would deter, or prevent, crime. The law was like a curfew law in that it targeted young people standing outside, but this particular law could be used by Chicago police at any time of day. The Supreme Court said that the law was too vague and that it harmed the rights of people who were doing perfectly legal things outside. Many other cities besides Chicago have antiloitering ordinances, but after the decision in *Morales*, they may be more hesitant to enact loitering laws as vague and intrusive as the Chicago law.

Apparently, curfew and antiloitering ordinances will remain a fact of life for minors in many cities. Do you think that these laws are a good idea? Do they prevent crimes from happening? Do you think that they get at the real causes of juvenile crime? Curfew laws often enjoy widespread support among adults. Do you agree with your rights being limited by adults who can vote, while you cannot vote to protest these laws? If you think that these laws are unfair, what can you do? You could try to work with other students and parents to protest these laws.

Racial Profiling

Police are not allowed to search people because they are minorities, or because they are young and male. These are not reasonable grounds to suspect criminal activity. Yet more and more studies have shown that police departments choose to stop or arrest people based on their race. These studies have shown that police tend to target blacks or Latinos and pull them over for questioning or stop them as they walk down the street. This practice is called racial profiling. For years, many people have complained about racial profiling. Lawyer Johnny Cochran, actors Wesley Snipes and Will Smith, football player Marcus Allen, and Olympic athletes Al Joyner and Edwin Moses are only a few of the people who have been stopped because of their race. Recently, after years of outcry, the New Jersey State Police Department admitted that it permitted police officers to target minorities by stopping them without reasonable suspicion.

How do the police try to justify this type of behavior? Many police officers deny that racial profiling occurs, even after studies show that many more blacks than whites are stopped. They argue that they stop people who fit a profile of many drug dealers or people who use drugs. Yet there is no correlation between race and drug possession. Even if the police are not consciously racist, they may tend to automatically suspect that minorities are criminals. The issue is very complex. As more attention becomes focused on the way police officers do their job, perhaps some of these discriminatory practices will end.

Many states have passed laws requiring police to keep track of the race, sex, and age of people stopped on streets and highways, so that it can be determined whether police officers engage in racial profiling. If you are ever stopped, you may want to observe whether the police are in fact writing down any information about the stop. If you have reason to believe that the police are targeting minorities in your neighborhood, you can take action. Many religious and civil rights groups across the country are involved in efforts to put an end to the practice of racial profiling. One place you can call is your local American Civil Liberties Union (ACLU) office, since the ACLU is part of a nation-wide effort to stop racial profiling.

What Else Can Be a Search?

Police searches include more than just looking in your pockets or your bag. Recording your voice, watching over your property, or taking samples of your blood are also searches. The Supreme Court has said that taking a sample of your handwriting is not a search, however, because whenever you write you give your handwriting to the public. Similarly, we leave fingerprints wherever we go, so when police take a fingerprint, it is not considered a search.

But anything that violates your bodily integrity is a search and must be conducted reasonably. Stomach pumping, strip

41

searches, and body cavity checks are generally unconstitutional when there are not strong reasons to perform them. Blood tests and urinalysis for drugs can also be considered searches. Breath testing is also a search. Any search that physically invades one's space requires probable cause or a reasonable suspicion.

A person's property is private, but if part of that property can be viewed by the public, the police can use information without probable cause. For example, a farmer in Kentucky had a fenced-off field, but police could observe marijuana growing in the field from the surrounding property. The Supreme Court said that "an individual may not legitimately demand privacy for activities conducted out of doors in fields . . . except in the area immediately surrounding the home."

The Supreme Court has also analyzed the issue of when people can search through our garbage. The Court has said that garbage is not protected by the Fourth Amendment because although it contains personal information, we have thrown it away and given it to the public.

Government Surveillance

Surveillance is one of the most troubling kinds of search because you never know when someone might be watching you. Supreme Court justice William H. Brennan once wrote: "Electronic surveillance strikes deeper than at the ancient feeling that a man's home is his castle; it strikes at the freedom of communication, a postulate of our free society."

Despite the protections that the Constitution provides, the federal government has often engaged in illegal

Despite the protection provided by the Constitution, the federal government has often engaged in illegal surveillance.

surveillance using electronic equipment or spies. These James Bond–type tactics were originally designed for use in foreign intelligence, to spy on enemies in the Soviet Union during the Cold War. But shortly thereafter, the U.S. government decided to use these same tactics in America, against communists and other political and social groups. For over thirty years, without any authorization, the U.S. government engaged in surveillance of the everyday activities of some of its citizens. This illegal surveillance was often carried out by the FBI in the name of national security, but was in effect used to ruin lives and discourage many people who cared about civil rights or liberal political causes. Today we look back in dismay at these abuses of privacy that were carried out by the government. These abuses were very much like things that occur in countries that are ruled by dictators or the military. People who believed that such abuses could never happen in the

United States were proven wrong. The history of the FBI program serves as a warning of what can happen if privacy rights are not respected.

J. Edgar Hoover ran the FBI during the Cold War—when he died he had been director of the FBI for fifty years. He was so powerful that presidents were afraid to replace him or prevent him from doing what he wanted to do, and several presidents granted approval of illegal FBI activities. Early in the 1950s, the FBI developed a secret program to fight the Communist Party in America, which was a legal political party. The FBI infiltrated the party's membership, spying on members and disrupting their daily lives. The FBI used CIA spy programs in the Soviet Union as its model. The FBI infiltration program was later called COINTELPRO, which stood for counterintelligence program. It was designed to function as a kind of domestic counterintelligence, which would "expose, disrupt, and otherwise neutralize" political groups the FBI did not approve of.

In the case of the Communist Party, the FBI sent people to follow its members and told their employers to fire them. The program resulted in countless ruined lives. This dirty-tricks campaign and the use of intimidation tactics destroyed the Communist Party and left many people—inside and outside the party—disillusioned. Some estimated that during the 1950s there were more FBI agents in the American Communist Party than there were actual members. Most communists did not seek to overthrow the government or use any methods which look radical by today's standards. Many people simply hoped to improve the conditions of workers, to alleviate poverty in cities, or to guarantee equal treatment for all citizens. Others were simply curious about the beliefs of the communists or happened to have relatives who had communist beliefs. It's hard to believe that people who were only trying to protect the rights of workers or help the poor were subjected to this kind of abuse.

By the 1960s, COINTELPRO had really run out of communists to attack but still wanted to continue trying to stamp out political views it did not like. The FBI switched its focus from communists to the civil rights movement. J. Edgar Hoover distrusted the civil rights activists who were asking for equal treatment for minorities. He decided that they were "dangerous" and that the civil rights movement had to be stopped. Hoover told President John F. Kennedy that Martin Luther King Jr. was a communist, and that there might be others in the civil rights movement. Hoover managed to receive permission to begin tapping the phones of King and other civil rights leaders. The intent was to declare war on the civil rights movement and, as Hoover said, to "take [King] off his pedestal and to reduce him completely in influence."

No evidence of communism in the civil rights movement was ever found, of course. The FBI agents listened to every detail of civil rights leaders' conversations for years. The FBI would use information from phone conversations to find out where King was traveling and then plant "bugs," or microphones, in the walls of King's hotel rooms. In one of the most horrendous acts of governmental abuse of power, Hoover recorded conversations King engaged in while having an affair with a woman who was not his wife. In a low point for American democracy, Hoover sent an unmarked "suicide package" to King which threatened that King should commit suicide or this information about his private life would be released. In this way, the director of the FBI tried to blackmail and cause the death of Martin Luther King Jr., the great hero of the civil rights movement. Hoover did this on his own, without the permission of the president. King knew that only the FBI could have taped his conversations and said: "They are out to break me." King had endured the pressure of constant death threats from hate groups like the Ku Klux Klan, but he was still shaken: Even the authorities were against him.

The FBI also listened in on Malcolm X's conversations. Malcolm X was a member of the Nation of Islam, or the Black Muslims. He was a powerful speaker and advocate for the rights of minorities, so Hoover wanted to ruin him or at least harass him. The FBI, as part of its program, purposefully encouraged disagreement between Malcolm X and Elijah Mohammed, the leader of the Nation of Islam. The FBI even sent false articles to newspapers describing fighting between the two leaders.

It is hard to believe now that the FBI, which is supposed to be part of a democratic government, would do such terrible things. But COINTELPRO continued for years. The constant surveillance continued into the 1970s. It became even more intensive when new groups like the Black Panthers began to form, demanding more radical changes to improve the conditions of the poor and minorities. The Black Panthers were torn apart by divisions because they never knew which of their members were FBI spies or who to trust. FBI agents would send fake letters from one member of the Black Panthers to another, and some of these letters contained death threats. Today, many antiwar and civil rights activists remember how they joked at the time about how they were

Radical political groups like the Black Panthers were subjected to illegal surveillance by the FBI.

being watched. As it turns out, they were not paranoid but, on the contrary, underestimated the lengths to which the government would go to prevent social change.

During this time of serious abuses of the right to privacy, the Supreme Court for the first time created some constitutional protections against government surveillance. In 1961, in *Silverman v. United States*, the Court decided that federal agents could not arrest someone based on conversations recorded in that person's home without permission. In 1966, in *Osborne v. United States*, the Court held that some eavesdropping is permissible, but that police must receive permission from a judge before they eavesdrop. Finally, in *Katz v. United States* the Court held that the Fourth Amendment of the Constitution, which, as we have seen, protects against unreasonable searches and seizures, also protects against eavesdropping. Eavesdropping is a kind of seizure—a seizure of one's words.

In 1968, Congress passed legislation in the Omnibus Crime Control and Safe Streets Act to try to give meaning to the Court's decisions by making clear what kinds of eavesdropping would be permitted. President Lyndon B. Johnson introduced the bill with a ringing endorsement of privacy rights:

> We should protect what Justice Brandeis called the "right most valued by civilized men," the right of privacy. We should outlaw all wiretaps—public and private—whenever and wherever it occurs, except when the security of the nation is at stake and only with the strictest safeguards. We should exercise the full reach of our constitutional powers to outlaw electronic bugging and snooping.

However, the law that was passed, which is still the law today, has some very large loopholes. Wiretapping and eavesdropping can be performed when any federal felony is involved, and consequently there is a long list of crimes where eavesdropping is permissible. The attorney general can also approve wiretaps or eavesdropping. Eavesdropping is also allowed when "national security is at stake."

How big an exception is the "national security" exception? Can the president decide that anything he chooses is a national security issue and that wiretapping is therefore justified? President Richard Milhouse Nixon tried to use the national security exception to allow the use of harassment and eavesdropping against whomever he wanted, mostly so-called radicals who he thought opposed him politically.

The Watergate scandal that led to the resignation of President Richard Nixon involved illegal wiretapping, electronic surveillance, and the violation of privacy rights.

President Nixon claimed that the president could eavesdrop whenever some national interest was at stake. In 1972, the Supreme Court in *United States v. U.S. District Court, Eastern District of Michigan*, held that even the president cannot wiretap without a warrant and that the national security exception is reserved for only the most dire situations.

President Nixon continued to illegally engage in some of the most infamous abuses of people's privacy rights in American history. The Watergate scandal that led to President Nixon's resignation began when his staffers were caught in June of 1972 trying to install electronic bugs and wiretaps at the Democratic Party presidential campaign headquarters in the Watergate building in Washington, DC. In the investigation that followed, the public learned that Nixon had performed illegal wiretaps of journalists and high government officials who were critical of him. He even had his men ransack the offices of a Los Angeles psychiatrist to try to obtain the records of a critic of his administration.

These abuses of the privacy rights of individuals by the president were only the beginning. In 1974, in the Senate hearings investigating the activities of the FBI and CIA under President Nixon, the public first learned the degree to which surveillance had occurred for years under FBI Director J. Edgar Hoover. Hoover had since died, but if he had still been alive, he might have used his power to prevent the public from ever finding out about the way he had abused the system. We finally were informed about the surveillance of Martin Luther King Jr. and various civil rights groups. Congress held hearings on the subject, and a lawsuit was brought by the ACLU on behalf of some of the civil rights activists whose lives were affected by the FBI's surveillance and dirty tricks. The ACLU won, and some of the people harmed by these wiretaps and dirty-tricks campaigns finally received some compensation, but only years later, and only after an entire generation of social activists and community leaders had their privacy invaded and were discouraged and afraid of the government.

4 Privacy of Young Adults

In general, young adults have much weaker privacy protections than adults. School officials can often search your belongings with less than the reasonable suspicion that police officers must have. Schools can sometimes disclose information against your will. And courts often permit parents to receive notice, or require parental consent if a teenage girl tries to obtain an abortion. The sad truth is that being young usually means having fewer rights, but knowing your rights means that you can protect yourself. There are things that you can do to challenge violations of your privacy, or at least to raise people's awareness of the issue.

Privacy and School Authorities

Imagine this: A student walks up to the school's principal and states: "Johnny has a gun, and he said he's going to kill

In an attempt to cope with drugs or violence, schools may invade students' privacy.

somebody today." Hearing this, the principal calls Johnny out of class and subjects him to a handheld metal detector test. The detector goes off. The principal tells Johnny to empty his pockets. Johnny empties his pockets, revealing not a gun, but a set of keys, which had set off the metal detector. But something else is also in Johnny's pocket— marijuana. The principal calls the police. They arrest Johnny, suspend him from school, and subject him to criminal prosecution. Imagine also that the student who gave the principal this "tip" knew that Johnny did not have a gun. Why then, would she tell the principal that he did have a gun? Because she doesn't like Johnny. Imagine further that at Johnny's criminal trial, his attorney moves to have evidence of the marijuana suppressed, only to find that the exclusionary rule somehow doesn't apply. Nor does it apply in the subsequent school disciplinary hearing. Sound far-fetched? Well, it's not. Not only have such scenarios taken place, the entire sequence of events—from the tip, to the search, to the admission of tainted evidence—is in most cases considered constitutionally permissible.

Like the police, school authorities may conduct searches that infringe upon your right to privacy. As you know, schools have increasingly invaded students' privacy with searches of student belongings, drug tests, and metal detectors. Schools are often allowed to ban weapons, electronic pagers, and cellular phones. Schools are trying to cope with drugs and violence, especially in the wake of Columbine and other school shooting sprees. They want to be sure their students are safe, but as a result, schools may overreact and end up creating an environment that is hostile to learning. Do you think that measures like metal detectors or searches make students and

53

teachers feel safer or do they create an atmosphere of fear? Do you think that there is a real crisis of drug use and violence in schools or is it a misperception?

It is legal for schools to use metal detectors. Perhaps one reason why metal detectors are so widely accepted in schools is that they are so common in many other kinds of public places, like airports and courthouses. More and more schools are installing walk-through metal detectors or using handheld metal detectors to check individual students. Schools are also installing video surveillance cameras in public parts of the school. Some schools even ask police to go undercover in the school, pretending to be students in an effort to catch drug dealers. Police may also patrol a school in plain clothes. A recent national program called the School Resource Officer (SRO) Program, run by the National Association of School Resource Officers, Inc. (NASRO), is working with schools around the country to place regular law enforcement officers inside public schools.

In *Tinker v. Des Moines Independent Community School District* (1969), the Supreme Court said that "it can hardly be argued that either students or teachers shed their constitutional rights … at the schoolhouse gate." However, students have fewer rights in school than they do on the street. The first time that the Supreme Court ruled on privacy in schools, it conducted a "balancing test" to decide whether a school's interest in finding out if students are doing illegal things was on balance more important than the interests of the students in having privacy. The Court ruled that on balance, a school's interests are more important. Over and over again, when courts balance the rights of students against a school's interest in safety, the court ends up on the school's side.

The 1985 Supreme Court case, *New Jersey v. T.L.O.*, involved a fourteen-year-old freshman in high school who was found sitting on the sinks in the school bathroom smoking cigarettes with a friend. In those days, smoking was allowed at this high school, but only in certain areas, and not in the bathrooms. The friend admitted that she was smoking and was given a three-day suspension. T.L.O, whose name was kept private by the courts, was taken to the principal's office and denied smoking anything at all. The principal asked to see her purse, which he had done many times. He searched her purse, and found cigarettes. Then he dug deeper and found cigarette rolling papers, marijuana, a pipe, and assorted drug paraphernalia, including a list of names and letters concerning marijuana sales. T.L.O. was suspended for ten days, and the police entered the case.

The government brought charges against her in juvenile court for delinquency because of possession of marijuana with intent to distribute. T.L.O.'s parents hired a lawyer, and the student argued that the evidence that the principal found in her purse should not be used against her in court, because it had been obtained illegally. She said that the principal's search violated her Fourth Amendment rights against an unreasonable search or seizure because the principal had not obtained a warrant signed by a judge.

The case passed through three New Jersey courts that each decided the case a different way. The case finally went up to the Supreme Court, since the Court had never before decided whether the Fourth Amendment even applied to searches by school officials.

Interestingly, T.L.O. was not excited about the Supreme Court hearing her case; by this time she had graduated and she did not want to be remembered for the rest of her life as the girl who was caught smoking in the bathroom. T.L.O., ironically, wanted her story kept private. Would you want something that happened to you to become an important legal case? Would you be excited that you helped to defend the rights of other students, or would you rather get on with your life and not have your story be in the public eye?

In 1985, the Court decided that students have "legitimate expectations of privacy" and that the Fourth Amendment does apply. But the Court also ruled that the search of T.L.O. was constitutional. The Court said that only "reasonable" ground is necessary for a school search, which is less than the full probable cause required for searches under the Fourth Amendment. While in some respects students have less protection in schools, school authorities are supposed to maintain a proper learning environment where students do not live in fear of being searched for no reason. On one hand, the Supreme Court said that school officials are different from police and that requiring probable cause would "unduly interfere with the maintenance of the swift and informal disciplinary procedures needed in schools." The Court held that school authorities do not always need to obtain a warrant to conduct a reasonable search. The Court also said that schools must consider first whether the search is justified, and second, whether the way it is conducted is reasonable, given the circumstances. On the other hand, the Court said that schools must make some effort to limit their searches so that they do only what is needed to find what they are looking for. The Court said:

> *[A] search will be permissible in its scope when the measures adopted are reasonably related to the objectives of the*

search and not excessively intrusive in light of the age and sex of the student and the nature of the infraction.

Some state courts have been more stringent than the Supreme Court; for example, Louisiana requires a full probable cause for searching students. Most state courts follow the Supreme Court, though, and require only a reasonable suspicion. Although school authorities are supposed to have a reason for a search and to make sure that searches are not too intrusive, many very intrusive searches have been allowed by courts. Courts are often deferential to school authorities, which means that school authorities do not need to have a very specific or strong reason to search a student. But the school officials do have to have some reason to search a student and must suspect that particular student of breaking a law or a school rule. They cannot generally suspect that some students are up to no good. They must be able to explain why they thought a student was doing something wrong. To make their case for reasonable suspicion, school officials can rely on things like a student's school record, information from other students, the seriousness of the problem faced by the school, or prior encounters between a student and school officials.

Some searches, such as mass searches and strip searches, are inherently very intrusive and might be more limited under *T.L.O.'s* rule against "excessively intrusive" searches. One school in New York strip-searched an entire fifth grade class because three dollars were missing, and a federal court, in *Bellnier v. Lund* (1977) found the search unreasonable. Some courts say that there has to be much more suspicion to perform a more intrusive search.

Searches of lockers and desks are also allowed. Since these searches are less intrusive than frisking a student, courts tend to permit locker and desk searches more often. Some state courts are more protective of students' privacy and say that the same suspicion is needed to search a locker as to search a student. A few states even have laws that protect students from random locker searches. Find out if your school district has a policy on locker or desk searches.

Examples of searches that are allowed

♦ The school security guard walks down the hallway and notices a faint smell that could be marijuana. The smell, he thinks, is coming from the lockers in the hall, or maybe a classroom nearby. The guard can, based on this, search the lockers near the smell.

♦ The school security team decides that there might be a gun or weapon problem in the school. They decide to spend an evening searching every single locker in the school without telling students what they are planning. Even a blanket search like this might be allowed, though there is no specific person under suspicion, or even any specific activity. Usually lockers can be searched only with a reasonable suspicion, the same way that your person can be searched only with reasonable suspicion. But some state courts are saying that lockers are school property, so they can be searched for any reason, or for no reason at all.

♦ You walk down the hall with a wrapped sandwich in your coat pocket. Your school has metal detectors because there was a recent incident where a student brought a gun to school. A guard notices a bulge in your pocket and rushes up to you, asking you to raise your arms and be frisked. Such searches are allowed—based only on what a guard may think is an "unusual bulge" in a student's clothing. But what if it is obvious that the bulge is not a gun? Or what if the frisk is conducted in a way that suggests harassment?

♦ You are outside near the school parking lot, talking to some friends. Students are allowed to talk outside, but it is unusual for students to hang out in that spot between classes. You lend your friend a CD that she has always wanted to hear, and a security guard rushes up to you, insisting that she saw a drug exchange. The guard, based only on behavior that is slightly suspicious, can probably search you under these circumstances.

♦ A school guard stops random students in the hallway with a handheld metal detector and frisks them with it, checking for guns or knives. You suspect that the guard is singling out particular students, but the guard stops enough students so that there is not a clear pattern. Some courts have allowed schools to use handheld metal detectors to scan large numbers of students at random.

• A principal finds two students in the bathroom without a pass. He suspects that they smoke marijuana and knows that smoking occurs in the restrooms. He asks them to empty their pockets and sees nothing except one student's wallet. He then opens the wallet and finds two joints of marijuana and one gram of cocaine. This is the scenario of an actual incident. A California court, in *In re Bobby B.* (1985), found the search reasonable, and said that it was enough of a suspicion that the students were in the bathroom without a pass and that looking in the wallet was not very intrusive.

Examples of some searches that courts did not allow

• A school principal searched a student who was repeatedly late to school and who was carrying a bag with an "odd-looking bulge." The principal asked to see what was in the bag, but the student refused to open it and said that the principal needed a warrant. In this case, *In re William G,* (1985), the California Supreme Court said that there was no reasonable suspicion. (But this case seems almost exactly like the situation in *New Jersey v. T.L.O.*, where the Supreme Court said that the search was allowed.)

• Twice in one hour, a student was observed going into a restroom, and seconds later another student would leave the restroom. A school official then conducted a drug search. In this case, the New York Court of Appeals ruled that this was an innocent activity and that conducting unnecessary searches causes students too much psychological damage.

♦ A school made all students participating in a band trip agree that their luggage could be searched without any reason. A Washington State court, in *Kuehn v. Renton School District*, (1985) said that this kind of mass search without any reasonable suspicion is not allowed.

You may have noticed that in some examples, there is little difference between some of the searches that courts allow and others that courts do not allow. The law is very divided in this area, and it may depend on your state courts' understanding of what is appropriate for officials to do in schools. So remember, school officials must have a "reasonable basis" for their searches, but usually just having some suspicions about a particular person is enough.

What happens if a search is illegal? Sometimes a court will not accept the evidence that police or school officials found during the search. This rule is called the exclusionary rule, since evidence that is found illegally is "excluded" from being introduced in court. However, the exclusionary rule probably will not apply for the purposes of a school disciplinary hearing, so school authorities can still punish you even if their search was illegal. Your school may have a policy that defines how they treat illegal searches for the purposes of evidence used in disciplinary hearings, so you can check to be sure how your school deals with this issue.

What Should You Do If You or Your Belongings Are Being Searched?

♦ First and foremost, be sure not to bring anything illegal to school. With so much policing and security in schools these days, it is a dangerous idea.

♦ Do not resist efforts to search you, since resisting police or school officials during a search can itself be a crime. Resisting can lead to a violent encounter, or just encourage an official to arrest you rather than perform a more limited search.

♦ Although you should not resist a search, do not verbally consent to a search. If you consent, then even if the search is illegal, whatever is found can be used against you in court. Say in a loud voice that you do not consent, so that other students can be witnesses to the fact that you expressed a clear refusal to consent.

♦ You should also remember that you have the right to remain silent if a teacher or a police officer questions you.

Police in your School

The scenarios discussed above involve school officials, not police. Of course, police are already inside some schools, serving undercover. Schools can also allow police to question students in school; often the school will allow police officers to call students out of class to discuss something with them. As with school authorities, you have the right to remain silent. And it is probably best to remain silent until you speak with your parents or a lawyer. Do not let school officials or the police pressure you into saying something that might hurt you in the future. If you are suspected of being involved in a crime, it is better not to talk to police or school officials; do not explain and do not lie. You should tell the police officers your name and address; otherwise, they may arrest you on the spot since they will not have any other way of finding you later. Try not to be intimidated if the officers say they will not let you leave if you do not talk to them or that not speaking will harm you. The best protection is to remain silent.

Some cities and states may also have laws limiting schools' ability to let police question students, sometimes saying that a school official must be with the student who is questioned to be sure that the student is not threatened. Some school districts require calling in the police when there is a crime on school grounds, especially drug or weapon possession. Find out what your school's rules are regarding police involvement.

Drug Testing in Schools

More and more schools are using drug tests to combat drug use. A drug or alcohol test is a kind of search. Like other searches, drug tests must be done for a reason; random or unreasonable drug tests may be unconstitutional.

The Supreme Court, in a 1994 case called *Vernonia v. Acton*, said that student athletes can be drug tested at random and without any suspicion because athletic programs are voluntary. Athletes are said to give up their privacy expectations because they volunteered to participate in the sport. Supreme Court Justice Antonin Scalia, who wrote the opinion, also said that athletes have less of an expectation of privacy because they change clothes and shower together. The Court also said that since athletes can be role models, it is especially important to be sure that they do not use drugs. The reasoning in *Vernonia* has been extended to include all other extracurricular activities.

Do you think that just because you participate in a voluntary school activity, that you should be subject to drug testing? Do you think if some students are randomly tested, that all students should be randomly tested? Does your school ever use drug testing?

The lesson is that courts do not protect the privacy rights of minors very well. Students can be subjected to a wide range of searches. Courts will often accept schools' arguments that invading students' privacy is necessary to ensure a safe learning environment.

Private Information in Schools

Aside from searches, schools are increasingly talking about releasing confidential information about students who they decide are "troubled." After the shootings at Columbine High School in Colorado and at other schools, many teachers have decided that for their own protection, and for the protection of all their students, they need to know in advance who the troubled kids are. They want guidance counselors to warn them if a student is having severe emotional problems that might be an indication of anger and violent tendencies. Teachers say that this will give them advance warning about possible problems and encourage more people on the faculty to get involved at an earlier stage in helping these students. On the other hand, it could mean that teachers will become unnecessarily afraid of students, or will develop unfair negative impressions of students. Releasing this information may also discourage students from ever visiting guidance counselors in the first place, since most students don't want all their teachers to know the details of their private problems. Breaching the trust between a student and guidance counselor may discourage students from ever talking to counselors in the first place, so it may do more harm than good. Students may be less likely to receive needed help.

Some school districts try to draw a line between the teachers' desire to know if they are in any danger and the students' privacy. Teachers are told if a student has made violent threats, what treatment the student is receiving, and how long the student will be suspended, but no other personal or psychological information. Again, privacy rights are balanced with other public interests. Do you think that this is the right kind of balance? Do you think that other students should also have a right to know if one of their classmates might have violent tendencies? Or that more protections for students' rights could be created? What role do you think the troubled student's family should play in deciding what information is released?

The Right to Privacy

What is your school's policy on releasing confidential information or records of conversations with guidance counselors? Do you suspect that counselors release information in your school? Ask a counselor what your school policy is. Or have your parents raise the issue at a school meeting.

After the Columbine shootings, people wondered why the school had not noticed that one of the students had a Web site with racist symbols, hate speech, and threats printed on it. Should schools be monitoring the Internet and watching over the speech of students? Should schools monitor use of the Internet on school computers? What about the free speech rights of the students? In one outrageous recent case, a school suspended a third grade student for submitting a fortune cookie for a project with the words "you will die an honorable death" on it. The student was just a martial arts fan, but the school decided that the message was threatening and that the student should be punished. Do you think that just mentioning death in school should be an offense?

The high school yearbook may become the next bit of private information that police use to combat crime. Police are increasingly using student photos from high school yearbooks in police lineups. Police show the yearbooks to victims and witnesses of crimes for identification of the alleged perpetrator. Recently the ACLU and other groups complained when the New York City Police Department collected yearbooks from all the city's high schools. Do you think that this is an improper use of people's images? Students never consented to have their photos released, but police say that when juveniles are suspected in crimes, yearbooks are the most comprehensive source of images of young people.

Some schools may release information to teachers from troubled students' private conversations with guidance counselors.

Student Records

You do have a right to access any records in your student file at a public school and also to stop a school from releasing your records without your consent. This right is important because otherwise there is a possibility that a teacher or school authority could threaten a student with changing his or her record or writing a harmful college or job recommendation. Some states or school districts have rules against teachers using recommendations to punish students for their political beliefs; teachers have written letters complaining that a student is politically active, antireligious, or does not respect the flag. These kinds of personal comments are inappropriate not just because they are harmful but because they discourage students from exercising the right to free speech.

The Right to Privacy

In 1974, Congress passed a federal law called the Family Educational Rights Privacy Act (FERPA), also called the Buckley Amendment. Before this law was passed, students could never see their records, much less find out if there was anything improper in them or stop the school from disclosing the records. Now, if you are a student and over eighteen years old, you have a right to "inspect and review" your records, and parents can also obtain your records with your permission. A school must respond to your request to view records in a reasonable time—not more than 45 days, and often much less, under some states' laws. Some records, like psychiatric records, can be seen only by parents and not by students. Students may see letters of recommendation, but not if they have waived the right to see them—many colleges ask that students waive that right.

Students also have a right to ask that incorrect information in the records be corrected. Students have a right to meet with school officials to have information corrected, and if schools refuse, students can request a formal hearing about the error. If your school is improperly disclosing your records or denies access to records, you can make a complaint to the federal Department of Education. The Buckley Amendment also makes it harder for schools to give out your information without your permission. A school can release information only with your written consent, unless it is just showing the record to another teacher. A parent can review a record before it is sent to a school to which a student is transferring. The Buckley Amendment does not apply to private schools, though. State laws may regulate private schools, however.

What You Can Do at Your School

Even if school authorities think that they have a reasonable policy, if you feel your privacy is being infringed upon in a serious way, you may be right. Even if what the school is doing is legally permitted, you may think that what they are doing is wrong. If students and parents express their concern over invasion of privacy, the school may change its policy. Bear in mind that it is difficult at times to challenge even an illegal practice of your school. While you have your rights, having those rights enforced may be difficult, and your principal or school officials may even try to retaliate against you if you threaten litigation. Of course, legal services groups or groups like the ACLU may be able to stand up for you. And standing up for your rights also benefits the lives of all students whose rights are injured in schools. As we have seen, many people, including students, have made sacrifices in many ways in order to defend constitutional rights. But be sure to think carefully about your options before challenging school actions, and talk about your decision with your parents and maybe with a lawyer.

Here are some other things you can do.

♦ One of the best ways to effect change is to start an ongoing dialogue about a problem. Discuss your school's treatment of privacy issues with other students and find out if people have been searched or have had their privacy rights violated in some way. See if others are concerned and want to help. Maybe the student government can get involved in organizing students or circulating petitions and information about students' rights.

* You could create a new student group or get together a group of students concerned about the rights of students. One good resource is the ACLU's "Student Organizing Manual," available online at http://www.aclu.org/issues/student/hmes.html.

* Decide upon an agenda. Are drug tests the problem, or locker searches, or use of police undercover officers? Is the school reluctant to admit what its policies are with regard to student privacy? Is there a particular school official who acts abusively toward students? Schools are supposed to create a safe learning environment for you. You have the right to demand fair and respectful treatment from school authorities.

* Have students sign a petition protesting a school policy or practice that you believe infringes on students' right to privacy. Set up a table with information about students' rights. Write letters or postcards to state officials or school board officials, explaining your concerns.

* Talk to teachers or guidance counselors who you think might be concerned or helpful; maybe they can give you advice about approaching the administration with a problem. If there are

teachers sympathetic to your cause, maybe you can get a faculty adviser to sponsor your work and share information about school policies and procedures. Also talk to parents; parents are very influential because they can bring up issues at PTA meetings or other meetings with school authorities. Parents should be very concerned about how students are being treated by school authorities and whether students' rights are being respected.

◆ Find out what your school's written policy is regarding searching students, conducting drug tests, or disclosing information. Not all schools have written policies, but many states require school districts to write policies regarding student discipline. Your school may be violating its own rules or school district rules. The county may even have a procedure in place for responding to student complaints, so you can get students together to make an official complaint about the actions that your school has taken. Even if no rules are being violated that you know of, understanding what the existing rules are can be helpful. You might be able to suggest changes to the rules that would better protect students' rights.

◆ Talk to a lawyer. Local legal aid or legal services lawyers may be able to help, or at least explain your rights and what your options are. Legal aid

71

lawyers can help only families whose income falls below a certain limit, however. But other civil rights, women's rights, and handicapped rights groups may be able to help.

• Contact your local American Civil Liberties Union (ACLU) office if you believe that your school is improperly invading students' right to privacy. Its lawyers could take legal action, and at the very least they can give you advice on what your rights are and whether the school is doing anything legally wrong. The ACLU's lawyers may offer ideas about other ways to help you defend your rights, like suggesting new school district rules on privacy or new school policies. The ACLU also publishes a wonderful book on student rights, called *The Rights of Students: The Basic ACLU Guide to a Student's Rights.*

• Talk to students about having a speaker from the ACLU or another privacy rights group come to speak to students at an assembly or a meeting. Students will have a chance to learn more about privacy rights and to ask questions in person about their rights.

5 A Constitutional Right to Privacy

The Fourth Amendment creates a right to be free from government searches, but privacy exists in other areas, too. The Supreme Court recognized a specific right to privacy in the Constitution very slowly. Today we have a constitutional right to privacy, but it is still unclear exactly what our constitutional privacy rights include.

The Supreme Court has said that the constitutional right to privacy includes rights related to controlling your body, especially contraception and abortion. Sex and intimacy are certainly among the things that we—and people in most other cultures—keep most private. So of all the areas of our lives, perhaps our sex lives deserve the most privacy protection. The most controversial privacy decisions deal with a right to abortion. Certainly, abortion affects the private lives of women in serious ways. Abortion involves a private decision about whether to bear children.

However, some people think that abortion is not private, because decisions of life and death, which antiabortionists consider abortion to be, are public decisions, something that the government can make decisions about in the public interest, and not something a woman can choose to do on her own. The question is what is a private matter and what is something that the public, or the government, should become involved in. As you read on in this book, think about whether the right to privacy as protected by the Constitution should be more narrowly or more widely defined. The Constitution is the supreme law of the United States. Maybe you think that the courts should be very careful about creating a new right where none existed before, since constitutional rights create such serious limits on the ability of Congress and the states to pass laws that conflict with those rights. And privacy is never mentioned in the Constitution, so perhaps a court should follow the Constitution's text to the letter and not protect privacy at all. On the other hand, we have seen how the people who wrote the Constitution cared about privacy, whether it meant protection from unreasonable searches and seizures or from troops quartered in people's homes. And maybe the job of the courts is to protect our rights and make sure that the Constitution adapts to the problems and needs of our day. Think about the role of the courts as you read about the Supreme Court's privacy decisions. These decisions are some of the most controversial and exciting cases that the Supreme Court has ever decided, and they raise many interesting questions about rights and what the job of the Supreme Court should be.

The first case to recognize a constitutional right to privacy was the famous case of *Griswold v. Connecticut*, decided in 1965. (Remember, courts had already recognized a common

The first Supreme Court case to recognize a constitutional right to privacy was *Griswold v. Connecticut*, brought by Planned Parenthood in 1965.

law right to privacy, mostly a right not to have people use your image or appearance in print, or to release your personal information.) The Griswold case was brought by Planned Parenthood of Connecticut, a group that was protesting laws that at that time prevented women from receiving abortions or using contraceptives. Planned Parenthood hoped to challenge the law that prevented anyone from selling contraceptives and asked a Connecticut doctor to help them distribute contraceptives and counsel couples in the use of contraceptives. The doctor and an official at the Planned Parenthood office were both sued and fined $100, and the lawyers for Planned Parenthood then argued that the doctor could not be punished because the law violated the right to privacy. They argued that married couples should be able to use contraception and that their decisions about whether they wish to have children are very private decisions that the government cannot interfere with. The government cannot regulate family size, they said.

Justice William O. Douglas wrote the Supreme Court decision. He said that although the word "privacy" never appears in the Constitution, the right is "implied" in the Bill of Rights. The Bill of Rights already protects against several different kinds of unreasonable government actions that interfere with our private lives. We have discussed the Fourth Amendment, which prohibits police from making unreasonable searches. The Third Amendment was discussed in *Griswold*, really the first time that the Supreme Court had ever discussed the Third Amendment. The Third Amendment's text protects against quartering troops in people's homes. However, the Court said that the Third Amendment also embodies the general idea that people's homes should be protected from unreasonable intrusions. The amendment is concerned with privacy, the Court said.

Justice Douglas also said that privacy is one of our "fundamental rights." The term "fundamental right" would become the term the Supreme Court always uses to refer to rights like the right to privacy, which are important rights even though they are not in the actual text of the Constitution. Justice Douglas suggested that the right to privacy comes from "penumbras" of the Bill of Rights. Penumbras are the lighter edges of shadows. A penumbra of the Bill of Rights would be a kind of shadow, or background, of the Bill of Rights. Douglas's use of the word "penumbras" was very new and confusing at the time. Many people still wonder what he meant. What the idea of penumbras really implies is that the right to privacy is in the background whenever we talk about other parts of the Bill of Rights, like the right to be safe from the police or the right to be safe from certain kinds of intrusions. The general right to privacy is not named in the Bill of Rights, but it is the purpose behind some of the specific rights that are listed therein.

Specifically, Justice Douglas argued that the right to privacy is part of the rights that are given to the people by the Ninth Amendment. When the framers wrote the Bill of Rights, they did not want to give the impression that the list of rights in it included all of the rights that people should have; the Bill of Rights includes only the ones they thought were important to list. So the Ninth Amendment says: "The enumeration in the Constitution of certain rights shall not be construed to deny or disparage others retained by the people." What does it mean for the people to retain rights? Can a court just arbitrarily decide that people have a right to something and strike down whatever state law it pleases? If this were the case, and if a court decided that drivers have a right to speed, for instance, courts could strike down speed limits. There must be some standard that decides which unnamed rights are part of the Bill of Rights and which are not. Justice Douglas thought that because the right of privacy was so important, it was obvious that it should be included under the Bill of Rights. He said that "a relationship lying within the zone of privacy [is] a right older than the Bill of Rights." In other words, the right to privacy is so old and so basic that it is an essential part of other rights that are listed in the Bill of Rights, so the Court must protect it. Are you convinced?

Even if it is true that there is a very basic though unwritten right to privacy in the Bill of Rights, what does a right to privacy have to do with adults buying contraceptives? The Court seemed worried about the idea that the government might search people's homes to find out if they were using contraceptives. And in later cases the Court also emphasized that decisions about whether to have a child or not are life-changing decisions that the government should not make for us. But does the Court's ruling that many decisions are personal mean that the government is obligated to let children buy contraceptives or allow contraceptives to be given out in schools?

Not all of the judges agreed that recognizing a right to privacy was a good idea. Supreme Court Justice Hugo Black disagreed with the Court's decision. He was very hostile to the idea of privacy rights and always argued that the Court should not recognize any rights that are not part of the actual text of the Constitution. He dissented in *Griswold*, which means that he wrote a separate opinion from the decision of the majority of the judges in order to express why he disagreed with the majority. He wrote, "I like my privacy as well as the next one, but I am nevertheless compelled to admit that government has a right to invade it unless prohibited by some specific constitutional provision." Many people still think that since the right is never mentioned in the Constitution, there should not be a constitutional right to privacy. Instead, they think we should rely on protections in laws that Congress and the states pass, or on the rights in the common law that we discussed earlier.

For twenty years after *Griswold* the Supreme Court developed the idea of a right to privacy and soon expanded the right to protect privacy in three areas of private life: childbearing, including the right to abortion and contraception; marriage, including the striking down of antimiscegenation laws (laws that stated that people of different races could not marry) and divorce restrictions; and education of children.

Why these areas? Laws affecting these vital areas of our lives "tend to take over the lives of the persons involved, they direct a life's development along a particular avenue," wrote Jed Rubenfield in "The Right of Privacy" (102 *Harvard Law Review* 737 [1989]). Reproduction, marriage, and education all involve important family decisions that change a person's life, and if the government could control these decisions, people would have very little freedom.

And yet, the government does make decisions that limit privacy, even in these special areas relating to sex and reproduction. Marriage is controlled by many kinds of laws that decide what a legal marriage consists of: Gay couples cannot marry, couples must be of a certain age to marry, and they must fill out certain forms and have a certain kind of official present. Once married, special tax rules apply to the couple. Education also has many restrictions; families must send children to public schools, unless they can show that their children are educated privately. The government even controls reproduction in some ways; couples are often required to receive certain medical tests to determine whether any birth defects are likely to occur in their children. As in other areas, privacy rights are always balanced between public interests and private interests.

Cases after *Griswold* often involved childbearing issues. In 1972, in *Eisenstadt v. Baird*, the Supreme Court overturned a law that made it a crime to distribute contraceptives to unmarried people. The Court said, "If the right of privacy means anything, it is the right of the individual, married or single, to be free from unwarranted government intrusion into matters so fundamentally affecting a person as the decision whether to bear or beget a child."

Five years later, in *Carey v. Population Services International*, the Court struck down a New York law that prohibited the sale of contraceptives to minors under the age of sixteen. The privacy right applies to all people, not just adults.

These decisions also developed the idea of a constitutional right to privacy. The Court held that the right comes from the due process clause of the Fourteenth Amendment. The idea that the due process clause restricts things that government can do is called substantive due process.

The Abortion Debate

These right to privacy cases culminated in *Roe v. Wade*, in 1973, and its companion case, *Doe v. Bolton*. In 1970, a woman using the pseudonym Jane Roe, pregnant and single, sued in federal court in Dallas, Texas. She challenged a Texas law that prohibited abortion and made it a crime except when "procured or attempted by medical advice for the purpose of saving the life of the mother." The case eventually went to the Supreme Court.

The Court ruled that women have a fundamental right to receive abortions, overturning laws in all fifty states that restricted access to abortion. *Roe v. Wade* is one of the most controversial Supreme Court decisions ever, and it is certainly the most well-known decision concerning a right to privacy. The Court held that a woman's right to privacy is a "fundamental right" under the Fourteenth Amendment. The reasoning that led the Court to this decision was complex.

One thing the Court did to reach its 1973 decision was

to review the history of the laws that made abortion illegal. The Court said that these laws were very new and that abortion had actually been legal throughout most of the nation's history. In colonial times, abortions were commonly practiced, and abortion had remained legal throughout the United States until the end of the nineteenth century.

By the 1960s, however, abortion had for many years been declared illegal everywhere in the United States, although some doctors still performed the procedure and some citizen groups were asking that it be legalized. In the 1960s, this movement to legalize abortion spread nationwide. During those years, advocates of legal abortion received increased support because of the tragic birth defects caused by the pregnancy drug thalidomide. An Arizona TV personality, Sherri Finkbine, had taken the drug during her pregnancy and was told that her baby would be born severely deformed and that an abortion would be necessary. Arizona required three doctors to approve the abortion, and Finkbine spoke to the press about her story, hoping to help other women to avoid birth defects. But when her story gained national media attention, her doctors canceled her abortion because they feared they might be prosecuted as criminals under Arizona's abortion law.

Finkbine ended up having to obtain an abortion in Sweden. Less wealthy women who wanted an abortion could not even afford to be treated by a real doctor, much less travel all the way to Europe. Because abortion was illegal in the United States, many of the people who were offering abortions, especially to women who were poor, were incompetent or not even doctors at all. Real doctors who were qualified to do abortions often feared they would lose their licenses if it became known that they were performing them. As a result, thousands of women died each year from botched operations or from the unsafe or unsanitary practices used by "back-alley" abortionists. *Roe v. Wade* was decided at the height of the movement to legalize abortion. The Court said that the right of privacy was "broad enough to encompass a woman's decision whether or not to terminate her pregnancy." This kind of right to privacy may seem more like the freedom to choose than the kind of privacy rights we have been talking about so far, such as the right to freedom from intrusion or from searches. However, a woman's decision about whether or not to reproduce is indeed a very personal one. If a state bans abortion, it is making that decision for every woman who lives within its borders, thus making a private decision impossible.

The Court weighed the value of a woman's free choice and liberty against the life of the fetus. The *Roe v. Wade* decision attempted a delicate balance and was very specific. The decision said that a state cannot ban or even regulate abortions during the first three months of pregnancy, which constitute the first trimester, and went on to say that a state can regulate abortion during the second trimester (the fourth, fifth, and sixth months of a pregnancy) only for reasons having to do with protecting the health of the mother. The point at which a woman's right to abortion ends, the Court said, has to do with the precise point in the pregnancy beyond which the fetus should be considered "alive." Traditionally, common law judges thought of a child as truly alive only at the point of "quickening," when the child first begins to kick. In *Roe v. Wade*, the Court ruled that only at the beginning of the third

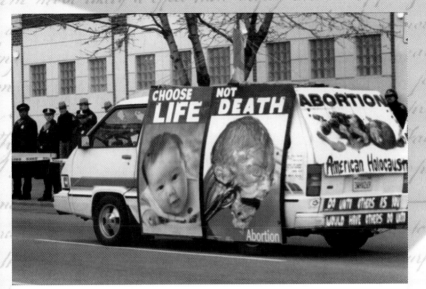

The Supreme Court's *Roe v. Wade* decision continues to be criticized and protested by some religious groups

trimester is the fetus viable, meaning that it would be capable of living outside of the mother's womb. So during this third trimester, the last three months of pregnancy, the life of the fetus becomes an issue, and therefore a state is allowed to ban abortion during this late stage of pregnancy. But the Court also said that abortion must always be allowed—no matter how far along in her pregnancy a woman is—when that abortion is necessary to preserve the life or health of the mother.

The *Roe v. Wade* decision has been and continues to be criticized by religious groups who argue that a fetus is a person from the moment of conception and that the life of the fetus cannot be sacrificed at any time. (Some religious groups would allow abortion if it is necessary in order to save the life of the mother.) But the Court said that until the third trimester the fetus is not a person and so the mother's rights should be weighed more heavily up until that time. At what point do you think life begins? Do you think that judges should decide when a fetus becomes a person? Or scientists? Or each individual? This question is still hotly debated.

In yet another kind of privacy decision, *Frisby v. Schultz* (1988), the Supreme Court held that a town can pass a law saying that protesters must not picket in front of the home of one individual. Large groups of antiabortion protesters had picketed in front of a Wisconsin doctor's home, shouting slogans and calling the doctor a baby killer. The Court said that the privacy of people at home is too important to be ignored and that there are other ways for a group to convey a message without singling out one person's home. The Court said: "There is simply no right to force speech into the home of an unwilling listener."

Some people who support the right to abortion think that the Court should have reasoned its decision in *Roe v. Wade* differently. Some think that the decision is too specific; it makes the Court seem like it is passing a law, not defining a general kind of right. Others think that the Court should not have based the decision on a right to choose or a privacy right. Instead, they see the abortion debate as really being about sex discrimination; denying women the right to control reproduction invades their bodies and forces them to bear children in a way that the law never forces men. Constitutional law scholar Laurence Tribe argues, "current law nowhere forces men to sacrifice their bodies and restructure their lives even in those tragic situations (of needed organ transplants, for example) where nothing less will permit their children to survive." If men do not have to give up a kidney to save their born child's life, why should women be

Margaret Sanger (1879–1966)

Margaret Sanger, one of the pioneers of the women's liberation movement, began the struggle in America for the right to reproductive freedom. In 1965, shortly before she died, the Supreme Court decided the case *Griswold v. Connecticut*, first recognizing a privacy right to obtain birth control. She began the struggle in 1914, when she launched *The Woman Rebel*, a feminist magazine advocating birth control; she had grown up in New York and saw the suffering of poor women on the Lower East Side facing repeated pregnancies, miscarriages, and abortions. She challenged the Comstock Laws that prohibited even giving out information about birth control, and she was indicted for obscenity and repeatedly arrested. She opened the first birth control clinic in Brownsville, Brooklyn, staffed by all female doctors, and though the clinic was raided after nine days, she won a legal battle to keep it open. She continued to promote birth control awareness, fought for the right to use birth control, and attempted to find simpler and less costly methods of birth control. She arranged for the first American manufacture of diaphragms and in the 1950s she helped put together funding for research that led to the development of the birth control pill. The writer H.G. Wells wrote, "When the history of our civilization is written, it will be a biological history, and Margaret Sanger will be its heroine."

forced to bear the hardship of bringing a child to birth to save a child that is not yet born and may not really be alive according to many definitions. Indeed, courts often recognize a right to control one's body, and denying only women that right seems discriminatory.

Other people criticize the decision from a scientific point of view. The *Roe* decision draws a line that places the viability of a fetus at the beginning of the third trimester; after that line the state can ban abortion. But what if, as a result of the progress of science, a fetus can become viable, or able to survive outside its mother's womb, much earlier in the pregnancy, maybe even from the moment of conception? In that case, would women lose the right to abortion?

Abortion Rights After *Roe*

The controversy over abortion rights did not end with *Roe*. In 1989, in *Webster v. Reproductive Health Services*, the Court dealt with a Missouri law intended to encourage women to give birth to their children rather than have abortions. The law banned use of any public facilities to perform abortions, and in areas where most people often used public hospitals, this might have made abortion services very scarce in large parts of the state. The Court said that the law was permissible, and that states can use their facilities as they see fit. Three justices also argued that *Roe v. Wade* should be overturned.

In recent years, as more conservative justices have been appointed, the Supreme Court has gone on to partially overrule *Roe*. Of course, many people think that it is wrong that important constitutional rights should depend on the number of votes a certain point of view can muster in the Supreme Court. Instead, many think that judges should interpret the law only as objectively and fairly as they can, ignoring their own political or moral views. However, for better or for worse, some of the Republican appointments to the Court were made using abortion as a litmus test, i.e. candidates were appointed only if it was clear that they opposed abortion rights and wanted to overrule *Roe*. The idea that judges should be impartial has continued, however, since even with many new appointments, *Roe v. Wade* has managed to survive.

In *Planned Parenthood v. Casey*, (1992), the Supreme Court returned to the subject of abortion rights. With five conservative Republican justices on the Court, many feared that *Roe v. Wade* would be overruled; and indeed Justice Scalia argued for overruling *Roe* in a dissent. Pennsylvania had passed a law saying that women must wait for twenty-four hours after receiving information about abortion before having one. Married women were also required to notify their husbands. These rules were designed to discourage women from having abortions without actually banning abortions; many other states were also considering substantial restrictions on access to abortion.

The Court did not overturn the right to abortion, but it did step away from the reasoning in *Roe*. One reason why the Court did not overturn *Roe* is that the Court is bound by precedent. This means that courts are supposed to follow past decisions except under very unusual circumstances. People rely on decisions of a court and want the law to be stable, so courts are reluctant to make dramatic changes in the law. In *Planned Parenthood v. Casey*, the Court therefore followed the precedent but made smaller changes in the law. The Court got rid of the entire trimester framework and instead said more generally that states cannot place "undue burdens" on the right to abortion. The Court also placed more emphasis on how the right to abortion is an important protection against discrimination. Abortion still receives protection as a right, and states cannot forbid all abortions. States now have an easier time, though, passing laws that make abortions more difficult to obtain.

Justice Harry Blackmun, who wrote the decision in *Roe v. Wade*, saw over the years how as more conservative justices joined the Court and support for the decision dwindled, abortion rights were only barely squeaking by. He wrote a defense of *Roe*, saying that "In a Nation that cherishes liberty, the ability of a woman to control the biological operation of her body . . . must fall within that limited sphere of individual autonomy that lies beyond the will of the power of any transient majority . . . This Court stands as the ultimate guarantor of that zone of privacy."

Abortion and Minors

In a case called *Planned Parenthood of Missouri v. Danforth* (1976), the Supreme Court said that states cannot pass laws that let parents prevent their children who are minors from having abortions. More recently, the Court has permitted some kinds of parental consent laws that do not give parents a veto but still make it much more difficult for young people to obtain abortions.

The Supreme Court in *Planned Parenthood v. Casey* upheld a Pennsylvania "parental consent" rule that says that an unemancipated minor woman cannot obtain an abortion unless she and one of her parents provide consent. Emancipated means that the woman is sufficiently mature or independent to make the decision on her own; a judge can make the decision about whether or not a woman is an emancipated minor. The law allows a "judicial bypass" option whereby the woman can ask a judge for special permission to have an abortion without telling her parents. This law even requires that the parent must listen to alternatives to abortion and receive state literature encouraging him or her to make his or her daughter have the baby. This law makes having an abortion especially difficult for minors, and many states have enacted similar laws. Other laws, called "squeal rules," require doctors to tell the parents of a minor about a proposed abortion.

Is the Court letting states violate privacy rights by forcing young mothers to have unwanted children? Giving parents veto power gives them control over the lives of their children. Do these state laws encourage more teen pregnancies, which hurt teenage women without affecting young men? Have you seen the effects of pregnancy on the lives of any of your classmates—have they managed to balance the responsibilities of childbearing with schoolwork, or has their education seriously suffered? Are these laws sex discrimination because they are directly harming women? Or do they just reflect different values regarding the life of the unborn, so that states should be able to target young women in this way, despite the rights involved?

If you want to learn about any restrictions on abortion in your state, there are many abortion rights groups you can contact. Planned Parenthood has chapters and clinics in most states and can offer abortion counseling as well as volunteer opportunities.

Marriage

The Supreme Court has said that the right to marry is a fundamental right. Deciding to get married is one of the most important decisions that people make. It is like the decision to have a child; it changes your life for many years to come. Marriage is also an important cultural institution, and it is treated as a sacred and momentous event in a person's life by many people. Marriage seems like an important kind of privacy right. Marriage also brings with it many privileges, like tax privileges, joint ownership, and the right to see your spouse in the hospital. Denying some people the chance to marry harms them very seriously—not only does it deny them privileges, but it makes them seem like less than real citizens.

Remember, the South did not permit black slaves to marry. This meant that they did not have the chance to make their relationships legal, to have the law recognize that a couple was bound together. One of the reasons that the equal protection clause was passed was to make sure that blacks would be able to marry. Southern states continued to use marriage laws to try to make blacks second-class citizens even after the Civil War and the passage of the Fourteenth Amendment. As recently as the 1960s, over twenty states prevented people of different races from marrying. These racist laws, called antimiscegenation laws, were often explicitly passed to protect "the purity of the white race" and to enforce a society segregated by race. The Supreme Court, in *Loving v. Virginia* (1967), held that states cannot prevent couples from marrying because of race. The Court said that a law that tries to do so violates the equal protection clause because it discriminates by race, and it also stated that marriage is a "fundamental right," or a privacy right.

The Supreme Court has also said that marriage cannot be denied to people just because they are poor. Many times, unfortunately, the ability to exercise a right can depend on whether or not you have money, and sometimes the courts decide that being denied a right because you lack money is too unfair to be permitted. In a case called *Zablocki v. Redhail*, the Supreme Court struck down a Wisconsin law which said that residents of Wisconsin could not marry if they owed any child support money. The law meant that poorer people who could not afford to pay child support could never marry. The Supreme Court argued that marriage is such a fundamental part of freedom that the government cannot pass laws that make it difficult or impossible for people to marry just because they are poor. In the same way, states cannot make it difficult for poor people to receive divorces and cannot require large fees to obtain divorces.

Right to Privacy and Homosexuality

There is an important debate in the country today about one group of people who are still not permitted to marry. Gay and lesbian partners are not permitted to marry, even though many have long relationships, adopt children, and lead their lives in the same way that married couples do. Still, some believe that marriage is meant only for a "traditional family" with a man and a woman, and should be kept that way.

Marriage also involves many financial benefits; married couples are given reduced taxes and special benefits. Gay and lesbian couples cannot receive those benefits. For example, if one's partner is sick in the hospital, many states automatically require the doctor to permit a husband or wife to visit the patient. Gay and lesbian couples cannot marry, and they are sometimes not permitted to visit their loved ones. In one famous case, Sharon Kowalski was injured in an accident and her parents refused to allow her lover, Karen Thompson, to visit her. Only after several court decisions could they finally see each other. Gay or lesbian couples may also have trouble gaining custody of children or getting adoption rights.

The Supreme Court has not ruled on permitting gay and lesbian marriages yet. But it is not likely that the Supreme Court's ruling, if it does consider the issue, will be very favorable to gay and lesbian marriages. The Court has said in its decision in *Bowers v. Hardwick* (1986) that states are allowed to make homosexuality a criminal offense. Many states have sodomy laws, which prohibit homosexual acts; until 1960, all fifty states outlawed sodomy and twenty-four states still do. Such laws are rarely enforced, but are often used to justify other sorts of discrimination against gay people; courts argue that if homosexuality is a crime, then gay people do not deserve protection from bias.

Such laws also force gay couples to hide their conduct from the public. The laws permit the state to intrude into private sexual conduct and seriously affect privacy because they force people to be secretive about their identity as a gay or lesbian. The nature of this discrimination makes the privacy argument more complicated. Being forced "into the closet" is like a kind of enforced privacy,

Gay and lesbian couples are not permitted to be legally married in the United States. The Supreme Court has not yet ruled on this issue.

and gays and lesbians want the right to publicly admit that they engage in private conduct.

The Court in *Bowers* seemed very reluctant to create new privacy or fundamental rights. It stated that "the Court is most vulnerable and it comes nearest to illegitimacy" if it recognizes new rights. The majority opinion also said that if the Court recognized a right to engage in homosexual activity, then a "parade of horribles" would come next, and the Court would have to say that other sexual activity is acceptable, too, like "adultery, incest, and other sexual crimes." The Court was not sure where to draw the line and emphasized that many states traditionally had laws against homosexual activity.

The Supreme Court did make a more supportive decision recently in a case called *Romer v. Evans* (1996). Colorado passed a very unusual kind of law. The law said that gays and lesbians could not be protected by antidiscrimination laws.

Any other kind of group could be protected, but not gays and lesbians. The Court struck down the law, saying that the state could not single out gays and lesbians for disfavored treatment. Some people think that this decision reflects a move of the Court away from *Bowers* and that the Court might someday recognize the right of gays and lesbians to be protected from discrimination.

What Do These Privacy Cases Mean?

Privacy is a right under the Constitution, but only in the three areas just discussed: childbearing (abortion and contraception), marriage (miscegenation and divorce restrictions), and education of children. These areas all involve very important issues, but we usually think of the right to privacy as being much larger, including things like protecting our conversations from eavesdroppers and being free from police searches.

How do you think that the Constitution should be interpreted? Do you think that the Court was wrong to create new privacy rights not mentioned in the Constitution? Some people think that because the Constitution is the supreme law of the land, courts should be very hesitant to create any new interpretations of the Constitution. They think the courts should have a very limited role and only follow the literal text of the document. This idea that there can be no rights in the Constitution that are not specifically written down is called "textualism." While many people think that the text of the Constitution is very important, almost no lawyer thinks that the text is enough on its own. One problem is that the words used in the Constitution are very vague much of the time and seem like they were intended to be interpreted by the courts. For example, the courts have to decide what an "unreasonable search" is because the Fourth Amendment just does not list all of the things that police can or cannot do—all it provides is a short declaration of a right.

Or do you think that we have to read meaning into the Constitution, but that we should follow the intent of the people who wrote the Constitution? People who care most about the original intent of the Constitution are often called "originalists," and Justices Antonin Scalia and Clarence Thomas are probably the most famous originalists. One big problem is that not only are the words in the Constitution themselves unclear, but we often know very little about the intent of the people who wrote the Constitution. And the Fourteenth Amendment, which was enacted after the Civil War, is in some ways just as important as the original Bill of Rights, since the Fourteenth Amendment made rights apply against the states. All of these privacy decisions are about things that states have done to restrict abortion or marriage. So should the intent of the authors of the Fourteenth Amendment be what really matters? And why should we care about intent? What if their intent was that we should decide for ourselves what our rights are?

Other people think that the Constitution was intended to be understood in changing ways over the years. These people think that the law should be flexible and adapt to new ideas and new problems in society. They argue that privacy is an evolving idea that changes over the years. Privacy is a more important right today because there are so many new ways that our privacy can be infringed upon. Privacy was not much of a concern when the government was very small and people led their own lives. Today, the government is very involved in our lives, and our lives are also more connected to other people—through technology, especially. The people who wrote the Bill of Rights could not have imagined all of the new technological or political problems that might arise, and maybe they would have wanted courts to adapt to new situations by recognizing new rights or extending old rights into new areas.

These debates over how to interpret the constitutional right to privacy are very important, and they reflect the same kinds of issues that the courts themselves are always forced to deal with when interpreting the Constitution.

Just because the United States Constitution does not protect everything that we think of when we think of privacy, that does not mean that we do not have a right to privacy. As we learned earlier, courts have decided that a right to privacy exists in common law. Many states also protect a right of privacy in their constitutions. And there are state and federal laws that protect different kinds of privacy rights. Many of the most exciting new areas in privacy law have to do with state or federal legislation, and not rights as interpreted by the courts.

State Laws Protecting Privacy

Many state constitutions provide greater protections for privacy than the U.S. Constitution. A state's constitution is the highest law of that state. State constitutions give you rights in the same way that the U.S. Constitution does, and although many people focus on the U.S. Constitution, in many ways, we have fifty constitutions and fifty legal systems. State laws can often provide stronger protection for many rights. States have their own constitutions, their own laws, and their own courts, which decide cases that deal with state laws. If your privacy is violated in a state that guarantees a right to privacy, you may be able to have state courts take action even though federal courts cannot.

Some state constitutions explicitly mention the right to privacy, which—as we have seen—the U.S. Constitution does not mention. In one example, voters amended Article 1, Section 1 of the California Constitution in 1972. It now says:

All people are by nature free and independent and have inalienable rights. Among these are enjoying and defending life and liberty, acquiring, possessing, and protecting property, and pursuing and obtaining safety, happiness, and privacy.

Nine other state constitutions also guarantee a right to privacy. Of course, courts must still decide what the right to privacy means. As we have seen, privacy means many different things to different people and can involve anything from protection from police searches and surveillance to abortion and marriage rights.

6 Current Privacy Issues

Privacy is in the news almost every day. People are constantly suggesting new laws to protect privacy because technology is changing so rapidly. Many of our privacy rights are not in the Constitution at all, but exist because lawmakers decided to protect our privacy by passing laws. Since courts have been very reluctant to expand constitutional protections for privacy, many people concerned about the right to privacy are encouraging legislators in Congress and in state legislatures to pass new laws to protect privacy.

Technology is providing us with so many new ways to live our lives, but it is also exposing our lives to new threats. For example, videocassette recorders have become very inexpensive, which has also made video surveillance equipment very common. Computers make it possible for us to shop and talk electronically, but they also make it possible for hackers to pry into our conversations and find out important personal information about us. More and more companies buy private information about us so that they can send us the catalogs and product information that they think we want. But this same information can be purchased or obtained by criminals. New technology may allow doctors to find out more information about our health, but we may not find it desirable that anyone with a computer is able to access that kind of private information.

Who Is Watching You?

In the last few years, many cities and neighborhoods have vastly increased the use of video surveillance cameras. The New York Civil Liberties Union recently published a map of downtown Manhattan with pins showing where video surveillance cameras are installed. The map was covered with pins; it is hard to walk anywhere in that area without encountering some kind of security camera. They found that on a typical short walk through downtown New York, a person appears on twenty different cameras. And this does not include cameras in stores.

Many of the new cameras are not private cameras owned by stores or security firms. These cameras are owned by the government and monitored by the police. Police find that they are an inexpensive way to watch parks or secluded areas when no police officers are around. The video cameras are monitored on a television screen in a central office, and the tapes are usually saved for a few weeks in case a crime is reported near one of the cameras.

The cameras have sometimes been shown to be effective in reducing crime (at least in the area in front of the camera). But many people who are advocates for civil liberties are uncomfortable with all of these cameras everywhere. They do not like the idea of the government watching our every move. Remembering the things that J. Edgar Hoover did, they wonder what would happen if the wrong kinds of police or authorities took control of all this electronic equipment that watches over us. Does your town use cameras to monitor public places? Do they make you feel uncomfortable, or do they make you feel safer?

Electronic Privacy

The police can tap your phones, but they are at least required to get a warrant signed by a judge to do that. Remember, even J. Edgar Hoover of the FBI needed President Kennedy's permission to listen to the phone conversations of civil rights leaders. Federal law does not permit private people to listen to your phone conversations or to read any of your e-mail. If you tape a phone conversation secretly, you might be breaking the law. The Electronic Communications Privacy Act of 1996 says that no private people or organizations, including employers, can intercept the wire, oral, or electronic communications of others. Many states also have similar laws. Linda Tripp, who recorded conversations that she had with Monica Lewinsky, was sued in the state of Maryland because she violated a Maryland state law that says that you cannot secretly record phone conversations.

Of course, if you have the person's prior consent, then you can record conversations. Some employers will include consent to have conversations recorded in contracts and employees may not even have read the particular fine print.

When you call an 800 number you will often hear a company recording that says, "This conversation may be recorded for your protection and to ensure quality service." Do you think that by staying on the line, you have consented to having your conversation recorded? Do you think that Caller ID is an invasion of privacy, or a valuable service that protects you from anonymous calls?

Cellular phones may permit even more serious invasions of privacy. The FBI is currently starting to use a new system that allows it to track the location of individuals through their cellular phones.

Computers and Personal Information

You already have zero privacy. Get over it.

—Statement of Scott McNealy, chief executive officer, Sun Microsystems, Inc.

In many ways, electronic surveillance is more troubling than a physical search because you rarely know that electronic surveillance is even occurring. Taping phone conversations is old technology, and new computer technology is much more powerful and more threatening to privacy rights. Justice Louis Brandeis feared long ago that numerous mechanical devices threaten to make good the prediction that "what is whispered in the closet shall be proclaimed from the housetops." The Internet has created an entire new virtual world in

Private information can be easily obtained over the Internet.

which the walls and neighborhoods and physical space that protects our privacy has no meaning. Computer networks manage so much information, make information so easy to access, and can store information in so many different places, that the Internet provides huge new opportunities for others to access personal information about you that you never even knew existed. The Internet connects computers to each other, giving experienced hackers access to private information in other people's computers. Millions of e-mail messages are sent every day, and on the Internet they travel through many computers before they reach their final destinations. Very few of the messages sent over the Internet are secure, and sometimes by "sniffing" computers along the way, other people can read your e-mail as it travels to its destination.

If you ever want to see how much information an Internet site can instantly obtain about your computer, visit http://www.Privacy.net/analyze/. This site instantly lists information about the sites you have recently visited, what kind of computer you own, what kind of Internet service you use, and who owns your Internet provider. And if that is just the information that can be obtained immediately from your computer, think of what determined hackers could do to access credit card numbers or more personal information.

President Bill Clinton proposed a "global information infrastructure" that would have some protections for privacy on the Internet. No such laws have yet been passed. Some Internet sites do provide information on privacy on the Internet. A group of sites have a program called Etrust, which rates sites based on their ability to protect the privacy of users. Technology for protecting privacy and ensuring that messages are secure on the Internet is always changing. And new technology is constantly being "cracked" by hackers trying to prove their skills, show weakness in protections, or do damage to sites and obtain personal information. Hackers have made a business out of stealing credit card numbers over the Internet, for example.

One way to keep e-mail secure is to use programs called encryption software, which code the messages and then encode it again when it reaches its destination. Most important to Internet commerce, encryption programs protect credit card numbers when people buy things over the Internet. Of course, even the most advanced encryption codes have been broken by hackers.

New Internet sites create new personal information that we never knew we had. A department store may keep records of what you buy in order to study consumer tastes. Many Internet Web sites also track the things that you look at. One Internet company is currently being sued because software that it gave away free to play music on secretly sent information back to the software maker, telling it what kinds of music people preferred.

Privacy rights conflict with public interests on the Internet just like in the other areas that we have discussed. With new technology, the government wants to assert its "public interest" in monitoring our lives. The National Security Agency (NSA) wants to be able to read people's e-mail sometimes, for national security reasons. The NSA and the Clinton administration wanted all encryption programs to have a special trapdoor so that the government could read everything. The idea was to create a government "clipper chip," which would be secure, but which government agencies could decode. The

Clinton administration said that this was very important to protect Americans from hackers around the world, and also that without the ability to crack encryption, the country's "ability to fight crime and prevent terrorism" would be "devastated." Terrorists might try to break into American computers to cause damage to Americans. But protecting us from hackers would mean that the government would have access to everything on the Internet and could monitor all information on the Internet at any time. Many privacy advocates strongly opposed this proposal, and the government abandoned the idea. After all, the government has abused such power so many times in the past, as we have seen in the last few chapters. Indeed, some newspapers have reported that the National Security Agency is working on a project called Echelon, which monitors private satellite, telephone, and e-mail communications worldwide. Once again, important questions arise about how we balance safety and privacy.

There are many groups that are working on computer privacy and Internet privacy issues. If you are interested, you can contact the ACLU or on-line groups such as Privacy International and ETrust.

Who Has Your Personal Information? Who Can Get It?

It does not take a hacker to invade your privacy over the Internet. A great deal of very personal information can be obtained legally, and this has some people worried. There are companies called data-collection companies that obtain private information about people. Why? They want to get lists of people who want to buy certain kinds of products, then sell those lists to other companies. Many of the catalogs and offers that you get in the mail are not things that you asked for; a data-collection company somehow found out about you and decided that you might buy something from one of those catalogs.

Data-collection companies are not doing anything illegal; they search information that is publicly available on the Internet. Often when people sign up for a credit card or when they order a product, they fill out a personal information card. They fill out their social security numbers, their addresses, and their favorite kinds of products, and do not know that this information will be made available or sold to other companies that collect personal information. Some people think that we should be warned that if we give out our information it will be distributed to all of these other people. The law does not yet require any warnings like that, though.

Selling information about people is a huge business. Credit companies make huge amounts of money storing information about whether people are a credit risk, including information about income, employment, marital status, court records, and past payment of debts and loans. For example, three large credit companies, Experian, Equifax, and Trans Union Credit Information keep over 400 million records on 160 million different people. One of the editors of *Business Week* recently signed up with two of the companies, and after paying a $500 fee, managed to get open access to their databases.

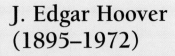

J. Edgar Hoover
(1895–1972)

Hoover is best known as the twentieth century's great enemy of privacy rights. He created the modern FBI in 1924 and was known as its director for life, staying in power until his death 1972. While initially effective at making the FBI a professional, disciplined law enforcement operation, he began to see his role as not just combating organized crime, but as safeguarding the morals and values of the country. In 1936, President Franklin D. Roosevelt asked Hoover to provide general background information on the Communist Party in America, and Hoover used the opportunity to create a domestic surveillance division. During World War II, illegal wiretapping and surveillance increased, even at the expense of investigating organized crime; the Bureau denied the existence of any national crime syndicate. He spent more and more time invading the privacy of citizens, trying to amass evidence to blackmail or intimidate people, including presidents, whose beliefs he did not agree with or who he wanted something from. He tried to keep these activities hidden from the public. He developed a partnership with the House Un-American Activities Committee, spying on and providing names of people in Hollywood whom he accused of being secret communists. In 1956, he created his counterintelligence program, or COINTELPRO, hoping to destroy so-called subversive groups using "dirty tricks." Hoover used COINTELPRO dirty tricks campaigns against the New Left, antiwar protesters, civil rights groups, black radicals, the Black Panthers, and other social protest groups. In 1971, a small FBI office in Media, Pennsylvania was broken into and some FBI papers stolen. A journalist received them, and alerted the public about the FBI spying on the Panthers, the antiwar movement, the Jewish Defense League, and others. Hoover died in 1972, just before completing his 55th year as director of the FBI.

107

For $15 a search, from his home computer, he instantly obtained credit information about a congressman and about then vice president Dan Quayle.

Even Social Security numbers, which are supposed to be personal numbers for tax collection purposes, are widely available. Companies buy this information and use it to create personal "look up" services, some of which any-one can use right on the Internet. There is even a problem with identity theft, where criminals use your personal information to assume your identity and apply for bank loans or otherwise profit from your information.

There is very little legal protection against this kind of personal information use. The 1974 Privacy Act limits some ways that the government can use your information, but it does nothing to prevent these private companies from distributing private information. In contrast, many European countries have very strict rules about distributing private information. The governments in Europe often take a very active role in making sure that no one is giving out people's information and that people are very clearly warned that if they give a company their information it could be distributed to others. Many people believe that the United States should have stronger laws, too, laws that make giving away personal information illegal, and laws that make the government investigate the ways in which companies use personal information.

Medical Privacy

The Supreme Court has not found any constitutional right to have medical information kept private. In *Whalen v. Roe*, (1977), the Court said that New York State could gather information about drug use by prescription drug purchasers. The Court said that although people had a privacy interest, the state had a strong enough reason to gather information on drug use.

Your school medical records are confidential because of a federal law called the Buckley Amendment, which we discussed earlier. But any records of a private doctor may be able to be accessed by others.

Consider these examples on the ACLU Web page for its Defend Your Data Campaign.

+ In Maryland, a banker accessed medical records to find people diagnosed with cancer. Once he identified them, the bank called in their loans.

+ According to a recent survey by the University of Illinois, 35 percent of *Fortune* 500 companies check medical records before they hire or promote.

+ A 1997 survey by the American Management Association found that as many as 10 percent of 6,000 companies used genetic testing for employment purposes. And the Council for Responsible Genetics, an advocacy group in Massachusetts, has documented hundreds of cases in which healthy people have been denied insurance or a job based on genetic "predictions."

Soon it may be possible to test your genetic makeup to find out if you are more likely to get certain kinds of diseases and conditions. Some are worried that this information might not remain private. For example, insurance companies might try to force you to undergo genetic tests so that they could charge you higher rates if they think that you are especially likely to get a disease that is expensive to treat. Employers might even fire workers who they think might develop some kind of condition that would make it hard for them to work. Yet even if genetic testing did become common, it might not be very accurate. Not only is information about one's body private, but one might never actually develop the condition or disease that the genetic tests predict. This would make such tests particularly unfair, if they were used to deny a job or health insurance. Legislation has been introduced in Congress to protect genetic privacy, but nothing has been passed yet.

Police are also collecting genetic information. They collect DNA samples from some offenders and can match the samples with evidence at crime sites, just like they do with fingerprints. DNA samples are very accurate and can be taken from something as small as a hair. All fifty states have some kind of DNA database collecting information on criminals. The FBI also has a national database. New York recently announced that it is building a huge database that will include DNA information for every person arrested in the state and every person in prison—not just violent felons, but people convicted for any crime. Supporters say this will solve crimes and will also help release innocent people who are in prison but whose DNA does not match material found at the crime site.

People concerned about privacy rights become worried, though, when some people, like New York City's chief of police, suggest that everybody should undergo a DNA test, even if one is not arrested under suspicion of committing a crime. Should the government be able to have records of everyone's genetic information? Fingerprints show a picture of the outside of your skin. DNA, however, contains genetic information relating to many aspects of your health and body. Perhaps some of that information should be kept private.

The Right to Die

One of the most private things is choosing the way one wants to die. Maybe the choice of death when one is very ill or in great pain is a privacy issue, a decision that one wants the "right to be let alone" forever. On the other hand, suicide is a crime, and maybe people should not have the right to have the power of life or death over anyone, including themselves.

Should we allow doctors to help the terminally ill end their lives? The right to die, as some call it, is partly an issue of technology. New machines can keep people alive for longer and longer, even if their brains are dead. Life-support machines keep the heart running, respirators keep the lungs working, and feeding tubes provide nutrients. So the systems of the body are kept functioning. But if the person will never wake from the coma, and is basically a "vegetable," then should hospitals or families be forced to keep these machines running?

There are ways we can decide for ourselves that we want to die. We have to do it before the fact, though. Courts have said that if people say beforehand that they do not want to be kept alive on these kinds of machines, then that is their choice. The people can write documents called living wills, saying that they do not want to be kept alive if they are brain-dead. It is their own private decision and doctors can then follow the person's wishes and decide when the time is right to disconnect the machines. Medical charts sometimes have the note "DNR," or "do not resuscitate." This tells the doctors that a terminally ill patient does not desire to have artificial respirators used to try to bring him or her back to life. But what if a person has not written a living will? Can family members make the decision for their loved one in that case?

What if people are not brain-dead or in a coma? What if they are awake, aware of their surroundings, but in very great pain, perhaps because of a terminal illness? Courts have said that people can commit suicide in certain ways, since people can refuse to take food or medicine. People can "passively" refuse treatment and end their lives that way. But many patients are very weak and therefore request that doctors assist them in ending their lives. This is called physician-assisted suicide. It is illegal. Doctors are required to take an oath that they will do everything to protect the lives of their patients (though they cannot force patients to take medication if patients refuse). Maybe the courts' prohibition on assisted suicide is wrong. Maybe for some people who are in a great deal of pain, it is the humane thing to do. Keeping people alive on these machines is also incredibly expensive. Insurance may not pay for it, and families may not be able to afford it. Families may be bankrupted, or the state may have to pass on these costs to taxpayers. A large percentage of medical costs in America is spent on the last few months of the lives of the elderly.

Should costs matter in cases of life and death? Do you think that in those cases where an individual wants to die, death should be a private decision for the person and his or her family?

The Supreme Court decided *Cruzan v. Missouri Department of Health* (1990) and held that there is a right to decline life-saving procedures if one is conscious or if one has written a living will. Nancy Cruzan was unconscious for seven years with severe brain damage after suffering a serious auto accident. Her parents wanted to end her life support. Missouri had passed a law saying that life support must be continued if there is no living will. The Court upheld the law, saying that there must be a living will or some other "clear and convincing" evidence that Nancy would have wanted to have life support terminated. The Court sent the case back to the lower court to decide whether there was clear and convincing evidence, and the lower court decided that there was enough evidence about what she would have wished, and the feeding tubes were disconnected.

Many issues are still unresolved. What if the patient who is unconscious is a child who never had a chance to express any wishes about whether he or she might ever want life-saving treatment to be discontinued? The Court has also said that adults can be forbidden from committing suicide. In *Washington v. Glucksberg* (1997), the Court upheld a Washington State law saying that doctors cannot promote a suicide attempt. Chief Justice William Rehnquist said that suicide has traditionally been illegal and that there is no privacy right to have assistance in committing suicide.

The Court was also worried that some suicide might be involuntary, that older patients might be encouraged to commit suicide. However, the Court said only that a law banning assisted suicide was constitutional. The Court did not say that states cannot permit assisted suicide if they so desire. One state, Oregon, since 1994, has already permitted assisted suicide in some circumstances.

Workplace Privacy

Some estimate that as many as 20 million Americans are subject to electronic monitoring at work. Most people spend a large percentage of their waking hours at work, so protecting rights at work is especially important. More and more workplaces have video surveillance and systems that can monitor phone conversations and e-mail. Employers use this equipment to watch over employees, fire them, or discipline them for doing anything improper, but also to monitor productivity. Employers argue that they have a right to know what their employees are doing. This kind of monitoring can sometimes be very helpful in protecting the rights of employees; if an employer notices that one employee is sexually harassing another with offensive e-mail messages, the employer can take disciplinary action before the situation becomes intolerable to the victim.

Many employers want to conduct background checks before they hire employees. Some ask for psychological tests, medical tests, or drug tests. Of course, there is an important legal reason for conducting these tests. Employers can be sued for "negligent hiring" if they hire someone who has a dangerous history, so they are sometimes required to do these kinds of checks. Day care centers, for example, are required by law in some states to be sure that job applicants are not a danger to children. Here again, there is a trade-off between privacy rights and public safety.

Employers can invade your privacy if they receive some form of consent from you—for example, in the hiring contract that you sign. They can listen to your conversations if they ask for your consent beforehand. Some employers may state in their employment contracts that you must consent to have your phone conversations or e-mail monitored. Some courts have even said that if a company has a well-known policy of monitoring phone conversations or e-mail, then employees have given an implied consent to let the company monitor them. Often the contract or employee handbook will very clearly say that all e-mail or voice-mail messages are the property of the employer and can be monitored at any time. Of course, many employees do not bother to read the fine print in their contracts or handbooks, so they may not know in advance that they are being listened to or watched. Also, the Electronic Communications Privacy Act allows an employer to access an employee's e-mail and voice-mail messages if the messages are on a system provided by the employer at work.

Drug testing is becoming more and more common as the government and employers try to stop drug use for safety, to improve performance, and to reduce health care costs. All federal job applicants are given drug tests, and many major businesses require random drug testing. The National Institute on Drug Abuse estimated that in 1990,

15 million Americans had urinalysis drug tests performed on them. Drug tests may be a serious invasion of privacy. Not only do the tests provide information on drugs, but they could also be used to find out other medical information—information on pregnancy, diabetes, or use of contraceptives, for example. Drug tests are an invasion of one's body, especially when blood samples are required. And there is some concern that the tests can sometimes be inaccurate.

The lessons to be learned from all of this are not to expect much privacy at work, and to be careful not to say or do anything improper on your computer or telephone. Be sure to check your company policy, but it is safer to assume that anything you say or type could be read by a supervisor. Many states have laws that restrict what employers can do in the workplace, but even those laws give employers a great deal of power to monitor employees. And if you are fired because of something your employer has discovered while monitoring a phone call or e-mail, your employer may not even tell you you were being monitored. Even if your employer does, it may be difficult for you to challenge the decision.

Privacy in Your Life: What You Can Do

If you are interested in learning more or working for privacy rights, there are many groups you can contact that work to protect different kinds of rights. You can volunteer to help during the school year or during the summer. Many groups will be happy to speak at your school or to sponsor student clubs. If you are interested in specific areas, like Internet privacy, privacy in schools, or gay and lesbian rights, there are specific groups that focus on those areas.

Preamble to the Constitution

We the People of the United States, in order to form a more perfect Union, establish Justice, insure domestic Tranquility, provide for the common defence, promote the general Welfare, and secure the Blessings of Liberty to ourselves and our Posterity, do ordain and establish this Constitution for the United States of America.

On September 25, 1789, Congress transmitted to the state legislatures twelve proposed amendments, two of which, having to do with congressional representation and congressional pay, were not adopted. The remaining ten amendments became the Bill of Rights.

The Bill of Rights

Amendment I

Congress shall make no law respecting an establishment of religion, or prohibiting the free exercise thereof; or abridging the freedom of speech, or of the press; or the right of the people peaceably to assemble, and to petition the Government for a redress of grievances.

Amendment II

A well regulated Militia, being necessary to the security of a free State, the right of the people to keep and bear Arms, shall not be infringed.

Amendment III

No Soldier shall, in time of peace be quartered in any house, without the consent of the Owner, nor in time of war, but in a manner to be prescribed by law.

Amendment IV

The right of the people to be secure in their persons, houses, papers, and effects, against unreasonable searches and seizures, shall not be violated, and no Warrants shall issue, but upon probable cause, supported by Oath or affirmation, and particularly describing the place to be searched, and the persons or things to be seized.

Amendment V

No person shall be held to answer for a capital, or otherwise infamous crime, unless on a presentment or indictment of a Grand Jury, except in cases arising in the land or naval forces, or in the Militia, when in actual service in time of War or public danger; nor shall any person be subject for the same offence to be twice put in jeopardy of life or limb; nor shall be compelled in any criminal case to be a witness against himself, nor be deprived of life, liberty, or property, without due process of law; nor shall private property be taken for public use, without just compensation.

Amendment VI

In all criminal prosecutions, the accused shall enjoy the right to a speedy and public trial, by an impartial jury of the State and district wherein the crime shall have been committed, which district shall have been previously ascertained by law, and to be informed of the nature and cause of the accusation; to be confronted with the witnesses against him; to have compulsory process for obtaining witnesses in his favor, and to have the Assistance of Counsel for his defence.

Amendment VII

In Suits at common law, where the value in controversy shall exceed twenty dollars, the right of trial by jury shall be preserved, and no fact tried by a jury, shall be otherwise re-examined in any Court of the United States, than according to the rules of the common law.

Amendment VIII

Excessive bail shall not be required, nor excessive fines imposed, nor cruel and unusual punishments inflicted.

Amendment IX

The enumeration in the Constitution, of certain rights, shall not be construed to deny or disparage others retained by the people.

Amendment X

The powers not delegated to the United States by the Constitution, nor prohibited by it to the States, are reserved to the States respectively, or to the people.

Glossary

balancing test   The Supreme Court often weighs constitutional values against each other and decides to balance different interests or rights.

COINTELPRO   The FBI's counterintelligence program. It was used against many political and civil rights groups.

common law   The oldest source of law in the United States that was inherited from the British. Common law is the law of precedent, which means that judges follow decisions in cases that came before. The common law changes slowly when judges decide that the old rules are obsolete.

curfews   Laws that restrict ability of people to leave their homes, usually during nighttime hours.

due process clause   The clause in the Fourteenth Amendment to the Constitution that says no state shall "deprive any person of life, liberty or property, without due process of law." The Fifth Amendment also says that the federal government can not deny due process.

encryption   Making something private by converting it into a code. Software that uses encryption is commonly used for Internet messages.

fundamental rights   Rights that are important, but not in the text of the Constitution. Fundamental rights include the right to marry, to have an abortion, and to obtain contraception.

Jim Crow   The regime of black codes and laws segregating African Americans which lasted until the civil rights movement in the 1950s.

originalism   The idea that in interpreting the Constitution, one looks to the practices and beliefs of the people who wrote the Constitution.

parental consent   Laws that require a parent's permission for minors who live at home.

probable cause   Cause to suspect the commission of a crime.

textualism   The idea that there can be no rights in the Constitution that are not specifically written down.

For More Information

The American Civil Liberties Union (ACLU)
Web site: http://www.aclu.org
The ACLU is a nationwide membership organization
and is very active in protecting privacy rights. The
ACLU has affiliate offices in every state and local chapters in many colleges and high schools. You should
contact the ACLU if you would like to help, or if you
feel that your privacy rights have been violated. The
ACLU's Web site has a great deal of information on new
developments in privacy rights, new cases, and new
laws that are being considered. You can send a free fax
to your Congressperson at the Web site to protest lack
of privacy rights. The ACLU's book, *The Rights of
Students*, is also available from its Web site.

The Center for Constitutional Rights
666 Broadway, 7th floor
New York, NY 10012
(212) 614-6430

This a nonprofit legal and educational corporation dedicated to advancing economic and human rights. The pamphlet, *If an Agent Knocks: Federal Investigators and Your Rights*, can be ordered from its address.

Cornell Law School Legal Information Institute
Web site: http://www.law.cornell.edu
Information about Supreme Court decisions on education is available at this Web site.

The Electronic Privacy Information Center
Web site: http://epic.org
This organization was established to focus public attention on emerging civil liberties issues relating to the national information infrastructure.

The National Association for the Advancement of
    Colored People (NAACP)
Web site: http://www.naacp.org
One of the oldest civil rights organizations, the NAACP has state and local chapters that you can get involved with.

National Center for Youth Law,
405 14th Street, 15th Floor,
Oakland, CA 94612-2701,
(510) 835-8098
Web site: http://www.youthlaw.org
This private, nonprofit law office, serving the legal needs of children and their families, publishes *Youth Law News*.

National Coalition of Advocates for Students (NCAS)
100 Boyston Street, Suite 737
Boston, MA 02116
(617) 357-8507
Web site: http://www.ncas1.org
This national nonprofit educational advocacy organization publishes *Steps* magazine. Each issue discusses a different topic relating to students' rights.

Privacy International
666 Pennsylvania Avenue SE, Suite 301
Washington, DC 20003
(202) 544-9240
Web site: http://www.privacyinternational.org/
This human rights group was formed in 1990 as a watchdog on surveillance by governments and corporations. It is based in London and has an office in Washington, DC. It has conducted educational and advocacy campaigns in Europe, Asia, and North America to counter abuses of privacy by way of information technology such as telephone tapping, ID card systems, video surveillance, data matching, police information systems, and medical records.

For Further Reading

Alderman, Ellen, and Caroline Kennedy. *The Right to Privacy*. New York: Alfred A. Knopf, 1995.

DeCew, Judith Wagner. *In Pursuit of Privacy: Law, Ethics, and the Rise of Technology*. Ithaca, NY: Cornell University Press, 1997.

Price, Janet R., Alan H. Levine, and Eve Cary. *The Rights of Students: The Basic ACLU Guide to a Student's Rights,* third edition. Carbondale, IL: Southern Illinois University Press, 1988.

Index

Photo Credits

Cover image: The Constitution of the United States of America; p. 9 © Reuters/Mike Theiler/Archive Photos; p. 17 © Hulton Getty/Archive Photos; p. 22 © Mitchell Gerber/CORBIS; p. 25 © Greg Gibson/AP Photo; pp. 27, 75 © Associated Press AM. Jewish Historical Society; p. 32 © Reuters/Jim Bourg/Archive Photos; p. 43 © Ted Streshinsky/Corbis; p. 47 © Bettmann/Corbis; p. 49, 85, 107 © Archive Photos; p. 52 © Associated Press WHEELING NEWS-REGISTER; p. 67 © Index Stock; p. 83 © Reuters/Brendon McDermid/Archive Photos; p. 93 © Reuters/Lou Dematteis/Archive Photos; p. 102 © Associated Press.

Series Design and Layout
Danielle Goldblatt